HYGGE TRAVELS IN COPENHAGEN

---

*An insider's guide to the best places
to eat, drink and explore*

HELENA SMITH

Hardie Grant

TRAVEL

HYGGE TRAVELS
IN COPENHAGEN

*An insider's guide to the best places
to eat, drink and explore*

HELENA SMITH

CONTENTS

WELCOME TO HYGGE TRAVELS IN COPENHAGEN

Hej!

Copenhagen is irresistible: its colourful houses, fairytale palaces, spacious parks and laidback inhabitants work a gradual but strong spell. Surrounded by sea, segmented by a wide harbour, dotted with lakes and sliced with canals, this is a picturesque and relatively small city. Alongside boating, cycling is a hugely enjoyable and overwhelmingly popular way to get around – the city feels, in every sense, like a healthy place and whenever I spend any time here, I don't know why I choose to live anywhere else. My favourite way to arrive in Copenhagen is by train from London, which sweeps travellers into the heart of the city and the timbered and chandeliered hall of the central station København.

Copenhagen has become renowned for sustainability, with lessons for many countries in how to live well and lightly. Good and thoughtful design is another Danish speciality, from ceramics to whole city districts. And the food scene, embedded in seasonality, is incredible, with many small independent eating places growing and foraging their food, and influencing restaurants globally.

Year round, but particularly in winter, Copenhagen puts wellbeing into action with the practice of hygge (pronounced hue-guh). In spiritual terms this translates as the gift of joy and cosy comfort. In practical terms it could mean the communal warmth of a sauna on a rain-lashed day, or the glow of a candle at a window.

Whether you visit the city for cutting-edge architecture, cosy cafes, elegant residential streets, transformed industrial spaces, canals, arty areas or the royal palaces, hygge will take hold and you'll embrace the feeling of living like a local ... just like hygge will embrace you.

I find Copenhagen a very easy city to love – it relaxes and replenishes me with every visit. I hope you'll love it too.

Helena

ABOUT COPENHAGEN

The site of the city was originally a small Viking village, then it became a thriving merchant's harbour – the name Copenhagen means merchant's harbour. From small beginnings the settlement grew into a hugely prosperous trading centre. In the 12th century Bishop Absalon built a castle where Christiansborg Palace now sits in the heart of the modern city.

Copenhagen became the Danish capital in the early 15th century, when its castles and legal, military and educational institutions were built. Over the centuries the city learnt to adapt and rebuild as it was hit by fires, plague, a naval battle with Britain, led by Lord Nelson in 1801, and German occupation during World War II.

The layers of history are still very much in evidence for travellers, starting at the very beginning at Christiansborg, where the atmospheric ruins of Bishop Absalon's castle – plundered and destroyed in 1369 by the Hanseatic League – can be visited. You can also walk treasure-packed corridors at Rosenborg Palace, peruse glowing canvases from the city's artistic Golden Age at Statens Museum for Kunst (National Gallery of Denmark), stroll delightful ochre-painted streets in 17th-century Nyboder and wander around the revitalised warehouses of Christianshavn, once packed with the bounty of Baltic trade.

But Copenhagen is no period piece. This is a city that for the last 40 years has been polled as regularly having the world's happiest citizens – the embodiment of hygge. Cycling is the way to get around, and there is even a term – Copenhagenisation – to describe the way other cities attempt to emulate the city's green approach to transport. Year round, the sports-crazy inhabitants jump into the harbour to swim, then open their pores in waterside saunas. And in a country where self-expression and mutual responsibility are embedded in the school system, human interactions are generally characterised by ease and charm. The average Copenhagener is multilingual, eco-conscious, sporty and sociable. What's not to like?

For all these reasons, and perhaps for others that you'll discover for yourself, it's a flourishing place, one that rewards and welcomes exploration. Hop on your bike and join the fun.

About

COPENHAGEN

ØSTERBRO

NØRREBRO

VESTERBRO

N

Key

1. Rundetaarn
   (Round Tower)
2. The Little Mermaid
3. Operaen
   (The Royal Opera)
4. Nyhavn
5. Christianborg Palace
6. The Royal Danish Library
   (Black Diamond)
7. The Circle Bridge
8. BLOX
9. Tivoli

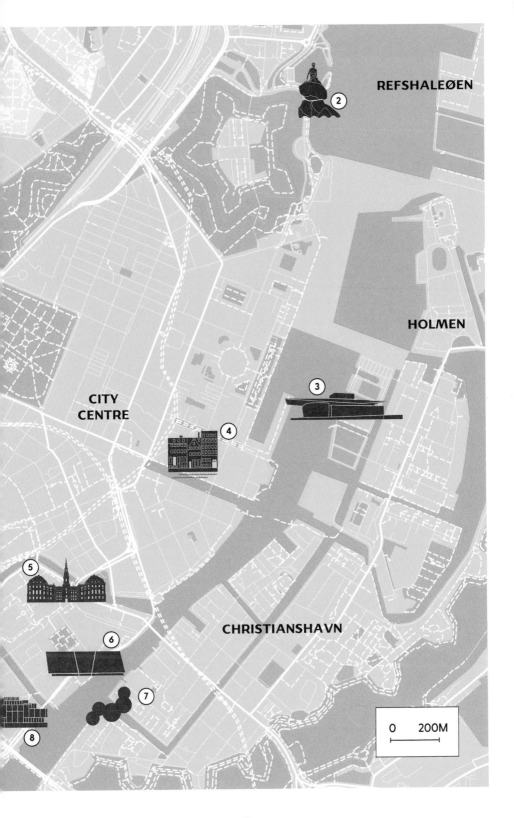

REFSHALEØEN

HOLMEN

CITY
CENTRE

CHRISTIANSHAVN

0   200M

NEIGHBOURHOOD INDEX

NEIGHBOURHOOD INDEX

NOTABLE
NEIGHBOURHOODS

Copenhagen is a small city and easy to navigate on foot or by bike. From the city centre, we explore the east of the city, before taking a counter-clockwise route round its boroughs, and then heading out to the far south-east. The entries within each chapter in this book are listed in this geographical order. Here is a brief overview of the very particular charms of each area.

CITY CENTRE

This was the birthplace of the city, way back in the 12th century when Bishop Absalon was given the town by the king and decided that the merchant's harbour would make a good spot for a castle: his construction was a fortress on Slotsholmen. The handsome and very walkable city centre now has a wealth of attractions, as well as great cafes and restaurants to fuel up in, from cosy and traditional to cutting edge. Amongst the unmissable sights are Glyptoteket (see p.95), with its abundant greenery and fine art, picture-postcard Rosenborg Palace (see p.103) and the treasures of Nationalmuseet (National Museum of Denmark, see p.105). To sample the modern side of this progressive place, explore Danish ingenuity and architecture at Design Museum of Danmark (see p.137) and BLOX (see p.143), or catch an arthouse movie at Cinemateket (see p.66). The sensual pleasures of the district include the humid Butterfly House (see p.120), where bright creatures flutter right by, boat trips on the spacious harbour (see p.91) and the glorious foodie abundance of TorvehallerneKBH market (see p.157).

CHRISTIANSHAVN & HOLMEN

There's a reason that tranquil Christianshavn, across the harbour from the city centre, may have you thinking of Amsterdam – the district was actually modelled on the Dutch capital. The artificial islands cut through by long canals were created by King Christian IV back in the early 17th century and stand as a wonderful example of city planning. Working class and naval Copenhagen meet bohemia at Christianshavn, and it has a very distinct and attractive atmosphere, as well as some imposing transformed warehouse buildings. The area's most famous sight is the car-free hippie settlement of Christiania (see p.113), while North Atlantic House gallery (see p.145) pays homage to Christianshavn's lively

Neighbourhoods

trading past. Neighbouring Holmen, a collection of small islands, was once the site of the royal naval base and dockyards, and has a long history of paper milling. It is now a centre of artistic creativity, featuring college buildings and the dramatic waterfront Operaen (The Royal Opera, see p.147).

REFSHALEØEN

Located on the island of Amager to the north of Christianshavn, formerly industrial Refshaleøen is a showcase of Danish ingenuity and creativity. From cool student homes in stacked shipping containers to eye-popping new building CopenHill (see p.149), a combined green power station and ski slope, the district is full of surprises. It's not yet on the metro system, but you can bus (2A) or bike out here, or hop onto one of the rugged harbour buses that plough up to Refshaleøen from Sluseholmen. What draws most people to the area, especially on sunny summer weekends, is sprawling global food market, Reffen (see p.52). But the surrounding industrial hangars host a wide array of quirky projects, including the ambitious Broaden & Build (see p.73) and Mikkeller Baghaven (see p.72) breweries, climbing centre Blocs & Walls (see p.128), Contemporary Copenhagen gallery (see p.150), and two sauna spots: rustic La Banchina (see p.125) and more zany Copenhot (see p.127). One of the pioneers is funky fine-dining restaurant Amass (see p.51), whose lovely allotment garden helps provide its kitchen with seasonal produce.

VESTERBRO

This soulful southern suburb was once the city's red-light district, and is now known for its mix of creative spaces, quality eating and nightlife, still gritty streetscapes and family living. A key cluster of interesting new businesses can be found in Meatpacking District (Kødbyen), where bars, galleries and eating spots have colonised the old industrial buildings. Leafy Sønder Boulevard exemplifies relaxed but sporty Copenhagen at its best: the long central strip of the street has been converted into a linear park, with basketball courts, bike routes and a nautically themed kids' playground. There's the Carlsberg old brewery and the Centre of Photography, and you will discover some excellent and unstuffy eating and drinking options, including the cocktail bar Lidkoeb (see p.75) and modern Mikkeller Viktoriagade (see p.77).

FREDERIKSBERG

Refined Frederiksberg is a leafy residential borough, where tree-lined streets reveal row after row of lovely tall apartment buildings. It's one of the most pleasurable areas in the city to simply wander. Frederiksberg Gardens (see p.129) provide a top picnic spot – the sweeping English-style landscaped gardens feature waterways with summer rowing and it is the location of Copenhagen Zoo. The nearby Cisterns (see p.151), a former reservoir under the lawns, have been turned into an atmospheric art exhibition.

NØRREBRO

Nørrebro is the coolest part of the city, hands down. This northern 'bro' has it all: modish bars, live music, directional vegan eats, eco shops, vintage treasure troves, affordable ethnic restaurants and the liveliest street life in the city. A great hangout is Assistens Cemetery (see p.131), where Hans Christian Andersen is buried; unlike its grimmer counterparts elsewhere in Europe, the cemetry is very much a used park. For shopping, head just north of the cemetery to Jægersborggade (see p.173), where the best shops in Copenhagen sit alongside cool coffee bars and excellent restaurants. By day you can cycle across wide Dronning Louises Bro (Queen Louise's Bridge, see p.130) and paddle a quirky swan boat on the lake, and by night join the locals and take a walk up Blågårdsgade (see p.79), which has the liveliest bars in the country. For a less boisterous night out, head for a natural wine at Pompette (see p.82), soak up some modern jazz at Sidecar (see p.84) or get hip to the city's live music scene at Alice (see p.81).

ØSTERBRO

Stately residential Østerbro is one of the greenest boroughs and its leafy heart, Fælledparken, is the city's largest park. This and the elegant 19th-century architecture makes it a family friendly place, a little low on major sights but high ranking in terms of seeing how the locals live. The big-hitter is the unassuming *The Little Mermaid* (see p.115), who looks as surprised as anyone by her own popularity. There's an arty attraction in the form of the avant-garde Den Frie (Centre of Contemporary Art, see p.152), and it's well worth pedalling over here on the weekend for a vegan brunch at Souls (see p.59), which has perhaps the prettiest plating you'll see in this famously foodie city. Nearby, Juno the Bakery (see p.60) provides cardamom buns par excellence.

AMAGER & ØRESTAD

The island of Amager is where Copenhagen comes to play, on the sandy strands of the eastern shore. The island contains Refshaleøen (see p.10), which we've listed separately. Amager has been called the kitchen of Copenhagen for its fertile soil, though there are new developments mushrooming here, including architectural marvel 8TALLET and the DR Koncerthuset (concert hall, see p.87). Otherwise it's all about the water, from harbour pool Islands Brygge (see p.133) to the curvaceous wooden lines of the Kastrup Sea Bath and the dunes of Amager Beach Park.

ECO CITY

HALF-DAY ITINERARY

When it comes to green living, Copenhagen has moved beyond cycling and recycling to reconceptualise how modern cities can function. This eco-aware route is, of course, best explored on a bike – just like a local. The well-marked separate cycle lanes make urban cycling a more healthy and hygge experience than it is in many other cities. Bring a swimming costume and towel for the chance for a sauna and swim on this route. If you want to partake of the tours at Hey Captain, make sure to book in advance.

9AM Hire a bike (see p.123) and pedal out to the once-industrial, now creative-cool area of Refshaleøen and breakfast on a fresh cinnamon roll and coffee at lovely low-key ① **La Banchina** (see p.125), where some of the produce is grown in the onsite garden. There's a simple sauna here, where you can sweat out any city impurities and, if you're feeling brave, then jump into the harbour water.

11AM After your morning refreshment, grab your bike and turn right out of La Banchina and cycle for a short stretch, taking the first right onto Krudtløbsvej, then left to head down along the water. The greenhouses you see ahead are used to grow produce for world-famous restaurant Noma, which is tucked away here. Before you reach the greenhouses turn right on Kongebrovej and then left on Danneskiold-Samsøes Allé to cut across the island of Holmen to ② **Christiania** (see p.113). At this pedestrianised and self-proclaimed free city they have been refining eco-living since the 1970s, and many of the homes are solar-powered and self-built. The area is notorious for the open (and illegal) sale of soft drugs, but you'll also hear some of the best live music in the city.

12.30PM Leave Christiania, pedal down Brobergsgade and turn right at the canal on Overgaden Oven Vandet. Cross over the small swing bridge and stop for lunch at ③ **Bridge Street Kitchen** (see p.49), where there are plenty of vegan and organic options, from around the world. Try the the healthy bowls and fresh salads at the California Kitchen stall, or veggie curry served on eco-friendly edible plates at Dhaba.

1.30PM Cross the large Inderhavnsbroen (bridge) and cycle down scenic ④ **Nyhavn** (see p.107). One of the iconic views of the city is the colourful mansions of Nyhavn; the street is pedestrianised down one side and the facing side is dense with bicycles which pour in here from across the harbour bridge. Turn right at the little bridge over the harbour and head down Toldbodgade to Ofelia Plads. Here the ⑤ **Hey Captain** (see p.91) company

does excellent and informative boat trips; by arrangement they will take you up to Nordhavn, a new northern neighbourhood where sustainability is embedded in every stage of design and construction. It's best to book your trip in advance, especially in high summer.

3PM If you'd like to make a personal contribution to a greener Copenhagen, go from Ofelia Plads up Sankt Annæ Plads, turn left along Bredgade which turns into Kongens Nytorv and then left again down Tordenskjoldsgade to the harbour. Cross the bridge to the (6) **Kayak Bar**, where you'll find brilliant (7) **GreenKayak** (see p.91). You can help clean up the harbour by heading out in twos in a kayak with a bucket and a garbage grabber, giving you a warm sense of achievement. Back on dry land, Kayak Bar is a perfect spot to relax, at one of their chunky wooden tables where you can watch the action on the water, and have a drink (from a corn starch cup) and a snack – most of their food is organic. Casual stops here can turn into big nights out, as they host DJ nights and bands.

Hygge is difficult to describe and, like pretty much every Danish word, it is tough to pronounce (hue-guh is as close as I can get). But when Copenhagen takes you in its warm-yet-wholesome embrace, you know you've been hit by hygge, and you will start to understand what really makes the city tick.

10AM Start with a leisurely breakfast wandering the fine food and fresh produce stalls at ① **TorvehallerneKBH market** (see p.157), where locals come to shop and graze on good-quality, often organic food. You could opt for comforting and healthy porridge at Grød, or enjoy a dose of African hygge at the colourful Ugandic stall, where the owner whips up fresh sugarcane and fruit juices.

11AM From the market, it's a short stroll north on Linnésgade to the humid ② **Butterfly House** (see p.120) in the Botanic Gardens, a celebration of warmth and nature that's the essence of hygge. It's a gorgeous sensory experience to stand amongst the blooms and watch bright butterflies flit by: they'll even land on you, and you can watch in wonder as the creatures emerge from their pupae.

12PM Exit the garden and take a left down wide Øster Voldgade. At the crossroads with Sølvgade, you can't miss the huge ③ **Statens Museum for Kunst** (National Gallery of Denmark, see p.93) ahead of you. Here you can bask in the glow of canvases from the country's Golden Age of painting: there are luminous landscapes by artists such as Johan Thomas Lundbye and Maritinus Rørbye.

1PM From the main entrance of the gallery, you can cut back through the Botanic Gardens, or go via the road and turn right onto Sølvgade, head along Østre Anlæg park and turn left at the crossroads onto Øster Farimagsgade. Walk along the edge of the Botanic Gardens, then turn left onto Gothersgade and right onto Rømersgade. Tucked away in the basement of the absorbing Arbejdermuseet (Workers Museum, see p.111) is ④ **Café & Øl-halle "1892"** (see p.31), possibly the most comforting and hyggelige restaurant in the city, with its cosy panelling, winking candles and welcoming buffet of traditional smørrebrød (traditional open sandwiches). As ever, the herring dishes are the most popular but there are also warming stews on offer.

2.30PM Rømersgade leads from the restaurant south to ⑤ **Ørsteds parken**, one of Copenhagen's many lovely and restorative green spaces.

Traverse the park heading south and cross Nørre Voldgade to go down Vester Voldgade. On the left sits ⑥ **Nationalmuseet (National Museum of Denmark)** (see p.105), where you can find out what makes this special nation tick. The display of doll's houses on a miniature street is particularly hygge-tastic, with lights glowing from their small windows.

5PM Cross Vester Voldgade and H. C. Andersens Boulevard to enter the southern gate of ⑦ **Tivoli** (see p.101). This nostalgic pleasure park is year-round hygge heaven, with strings of lanterns, painted merry-go-rounds and foliage-shrouded restaurants and bars. There's a plethora of heart-stopping rides, but you can also have a mellow and very cosy time here. Take a little boat for two onto the lake and enjoy the beautiful Hans Christian Andersen ride, called Den Flyvende Kuffert (The Flying Trunk), which takes you on a gentle rollercoaster trip through the wonderful world of his fairytales.

6.30PM There's no need to exit Tivoli for dinner, as there are some excellent options here. Try earthy ⑧ **Groften**, which dates back to 1874 and features jolly aproned waiters, fairy lights and red-checked tablecloths. Or you can choose from a range of cuisines at the ⑨ **Tivoli Food Hall** (see p.37). And then stroll the paths and watch the lamps and illuminations come to life.

9PM One of the best spots in town for a hygge nightcap is old-school bar ⑩ **Palae** (see p.67), which will take you in its warm and somewhat drunken embrace. It's about a 10-minute journey by car from Tivoli, or a 20-minute stroll along Vesterbrogade, across the pedestrian crossing to Strøget, and following it to Ny Østergade, turning left, then right on to Grønnegade, and right on to Ny Adelgade.

*Copenhagen is a youthful, energetic city that knows how to enjoy itself.
The district of Nørrebro overflows with creativity and fun and is well
worth at least half a day of your time.*

1PM Start your afternoon with lunch at ① **Manfreds** (see p.57), a farm-to-table restaurant that does a good line in natural wines.

2.30PM Manfreds sits on the best shopping street in the city, the attractive boulevard of ② **Jægersborggade** (see p.173), which is lined with colourful and imaginative stores: head to LØS Market (no.20) for unpackaged and organic food, Palermo Hollywood (no.31) for gorgeous recycled vintage pieces and Ladyfingers (no.4) for minimalist jewellery.

3.30PM Head south down Jægersborggade and cross over Jagtvej at the end of the street to enter ③ **Assistens Cemetery** (see p.131), walking down its wide poplar-lined avenue. It's the resting place of distinguished Danes, but this is also where the neighbourhood's locals come to lounge and play on warm days. Turn left to exit the cemetery, go right on Nørrebrogade and, just after the point where the cemetery wall stops, cross over to stylish ④ **Andersen & Maillard** (see p.56) for a barista-made coffee.

5PM Continue down Nørrebrogade for another block, then left onto leafy and lovely Elmegade, branching left onto Birkegade to check out some imaginative stores: ⑤ **BauBau** (see p.175) sells second-hand designer menswear, and you'll find quirky upcycled fashion for women at ⑥ **Muttilove** (see p.174).

6PM At the top of the street make a sharp right onto Egegade, take a left back onto Elmegade, take the first right on Sankt Hans Torv and then turn right again to stroll down wide Fælledvej. Have dinner at funky ⑦ **Plant Power Food** (see p.55), where they create delicious, colourful vegan dishes.

8PM Turn left out of Plant Power Food to go back up Fælledvej, then curve left on Nørre Allé. Look out on the left for the alley leading to ⑧ **Alice** (see p.81), where there are nearly nightly gigs – it's worth taking a chance on anything they programme here.

10.30PM Go back down past Plant Power Food and cross Nørrebrogade to reach ⑨ **Blågårdsgade** (see p.79), lined with cool cafes and restaurants, and at night hundreds of parked bicycles belonging to the partying locals.

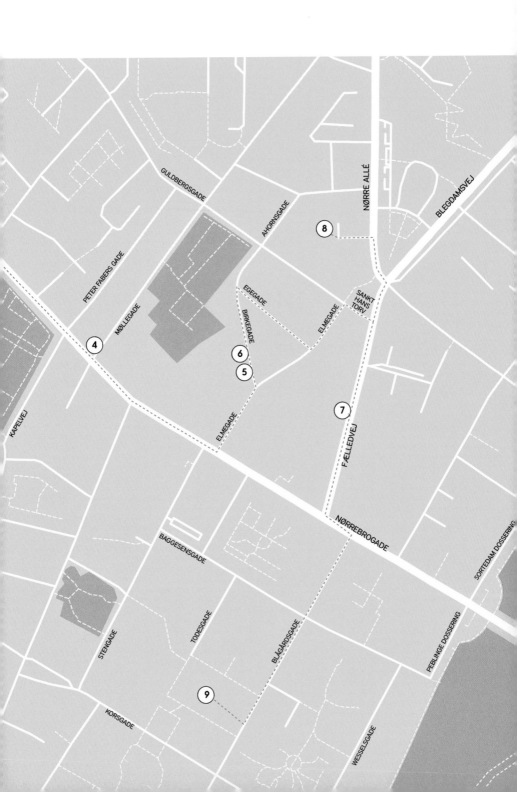

WEEKEND VIBE

FULL-DAY ITINERARY

This itinerary has a distinctly weekend vibe and gives you a feel for how locals like to spend a leisurely day off. The route is best experienced by bike and, in addition to plenty of cycling, includes brunch and a swim spot – bring a swimming costume and towel – for a full dose of Danish authenticity.

10AM Brunch is a quintessential Copenhagen experience, and my favourite option for its enchantingly pretty plating is ① **Souls** (see p.59) in the residential district of Østerbro. Its elongated dishes are piled with dainty but satisfying servings of scrambled tofu, sourdough with hummus, chocolate-dipped strawberries, pancakes with blackberry, apple and cardamom compote, and lavender and blackberry overnight oats topped with homemade pear and rosehip jam. Pedal over here, up spacious avenues lined by tall apartment buildings.

12PM From Souls turn left onto Marstalsgade, go left again onto Hobrogade and then take the first right onto Nordre Frihavnsgade. At the major junction of Trianglen, take a right onto Østerbrogade, leaving the street where it meets the lake on your right-hand side. This is a leafy stretch, as you cycle along the water, under Fredensbro (bridge) to ② **Dronning Louises Bro** (Queen Louise's Bridge, see p.130). This bridge is thick with cyclists at most times of day, and is a favourite meeting point for Copenhagen folk. Just beyond the bridge is a little jetty, from where you can take cute swan-shaped pedalos onto the water.

2PM Moving on, cycle across the bridge, turn right for a few metres, then left onto Vendersgade and cross Nørre Voldgade to continue south on Nørregade. Eventually you pass Huset culture house to your left (see p.26), with its vertical neon sign. Cross the water just beyond Huset to reach the little island of Slotsholmen. Continuing the soulful local theme, this is where the city began. There are a host of attractions on this compact piece of land, but one of the best is the underground ruins at ③ **Christiansborg Palace** (see p.97) – the palace itself is rather theatrically pompous, but underneath you can walk the remnants of Bishop Absalon's 1167 castle, the first major building in the city. The islet is also the site of the ochre-painted temple that houses ④ **Thorvaldsens Museum**, displaying work by the country's best-known sculptor. You also can't miss the dramatic polished granite ⑤ **Royal Danish Library** (Black Diamond, see p.139), which houses the city's royal library and hosts exhibitions.

WEEKEND VIBE

4PM Near the Black Diamond, there's a stop for the yellow ⑥ **harbour bus boats** (see p.91). Plying up and down the waters, these bright boats are as cheap as an ordinary bus and are a hugely quick and handy way of taking a trip down the wide harbour – you can even take your bike on board. (The itinerary returns to the same spot though, so it's better to lock up your bike at the ferry stop, unless you're considering cycling back over a bridge to this point.) It takes just a few minutes to cross over the water on the harbour bus to ⑦ **Islands Brygge** (see p.133), where there's a fabulous harbour pool complete with a distinctive red and white striped column and a diving board. It's one of the city's most attractive swimming spots.

6PM Hop back on the harbour bus, landing back at Slotsholmen, from where it's a short pedal back to ⑧ **Huset** (see p.65), which you passed earlier in the day. This tall and ancient building has been providing happy nights out for the city since 1970, with a board games cafe, cinema, bar, music venue and affordable, affable bistro-style restaurant. You can spend your whole evening here before pedalling via a well-lit cycle lane back to your accommodation.

9PM If you feel like staying out, seek out one of the neighbourhood bars which do great weekend jazz nights. Try brilliant backstreet cocktail bar ⑨ **Sidecar**, which has live music every Sunday night. It's about a 10-minute cycle or a 30-minute walk along Gyldenløvesgade and Aboulevard, veering right onto Rantzausgade, and turning right on to Skyttegade.

SMØRREBRØD
+ MORE

Smørrebrød is the traditional Danish open sandwich on rye, and remains exceptionally popular – especially when washed down with craft beer, aquavit spirit or snaps. Herring is a popular choice but the combinations are pretty much endless, whether you're in an old-fashioned checked-tablecloth joint or a more modern one. But Copenhagen isn't all about smørrebrød.

Boasting creative chefs and ultra-seasonal and imaginative eating, the city is a serious foodie destination. This chapter features places that embody the very Copenhagen approach of sourcing ingredients from onsite kitchen gardens, like sensational Amass (see p.51), and serving food in spectacular settings, such as the greenhouse of Vækst (see p.43) or street-eat markets: Reffen (see p.52) and Bridge Street Kitchen (see p.49), with their spectacular waterfront views. The best restaurant in the world is here, too – Noma – which, given the months' long waiting list, isn't included, but book ahead if you can.

Café & Øl-halle "1892"

Old-school eating at a traditional beer hall.

This basement beer hall is Copenhagen at its most enticingly old-fashioned, and I find it hygge-irresistible. Located downstairs from Arbejdermuseet (The Workers Museum, see p.111), it is a 19th-century time capsule: candles wink in their brass holders, walls are wood-panelled, perky traditional songs float from the speakers and the central buffet table groans with little powder-blue plates of dainty smørrebrød.

Each day the chefs concoct an amazing 22 varieties of traditional smørrebrød, with the usual pickled herring as well as eggs, pork, shrimp, beef, salmon and steak tartare. Pick up whatever catches your eye and take it to your individual table, where an aproned waiter will take your drink order: homebrewed beer, aquavit or snaps. The food is fresh and delicately flavoursome, with organic vegetables, free-range meat and fish that comes from sustainable sources. The all-you-can-eat buffet also features hot dishes, such as roast pork and tartelettes with free-range chicken, as well as cheeses, pickles and rye bread. You can order individual items from the lunch menu, but I find the best option in this pricey city is to fuel up for the rest of the day at the buffet, which will have you coming back for more. And more.

	⊙	**DKK**
Rømersgade 22	Mon–Sat 11am–5pm	199
33 33 00 18		
		W
		cafeogoelhalle.dk
Nørreport		

Smørrebrød + more

Klint

*Chic eats at Design
Museum Danmark.*

Bredgade 68

33 18 56 56

Marmorkirken

Tues & Thur–Sun 10am–6pm
Wed 10am–9pm

DKK

140

W

designmuseum.dk

As befits the cafe at the Design Museum
Danmark (see p.137), this is a stylish
lunch spot where you can enjoy traditional
smørrebrød with a modern twist. Sample the
rye bread piled with beetroot-infused salmon,
clouds of fluffy cheese and a feathery
topping of dill, or go for Norwegian Karrysild
(herring in curry dressing), with capers and
red grapes. Sweet treats include rich nutty
truffles and lemon and blueberry cakes.

You can eat under the tall linden trees
on the cobbled courtyard terrace, wrapped up
in a blanket if the air is chilly, or stay inside
under the rows of 1944 Kaare Klint lanterns
in the salon. Here you'll be sitting, of course,
on an Arne Jacobsen chair: the 1957 Grand
Prix in coloured ash with chrome legs.

You don't need to pay the museum
admission to enter the cafe.

Aamanns 1921

Elegant eating in the old town.

Niels Hemmingsens Gade 19–21

20 80 52 04

Nørreport / Kongens Nytorv

Sun–Mon 11.30am–3pm
Tues–Sat 11.30am–3pm
& 6–9.30pm

DKK
110–150

W
aamanns.dk

Aamanns is city centre modern elegance at its best: it's housed in a low, modern building cleverly tucked between ochre-timbered mansions. The interior is very beautiful, with tiled floors, rugged concrete walls and low lanterns, and the chairs bring alot of hygge, they take you in their wooden embrace, are thickly cushioned and with warming throw blankets generously scattered around.

This is another utterly classic place for smørrebrød but with more of an upmarket air than most. And, a bit like the decor, the food combines traditional and contemporary influences. Sandwich dishes include chicken salad with porcini mushrooms, and hay-baked beetroots with lovage, crispy buckwheat and horseradish. In the evening the restaurant moves beyond smørrebrød: the cured scallop dish with buttermilk, oysters, fermented asparagus and lovage is just one of their esoteric menu choices. Round off your meal with a sublime chocolate cake with rose sorbet and sea buckthorn.

Smørrebrød + more

Apollo Bar

*Mingle with the arty crowd at this
Nyhavn gem.*

When the crowds at Nyhavn (see p.107) get too much, I duck into the quiet courtyard of Kunsthal Charlottenborg (see p.140), where Apollo is an understated and stylish spot for a breakfast coffee and blueberry and ricotta toast or yoghurt with pumpkin and granola. Pastries bedeck the granite counter, cushioned blue benches line the walls and a dramatic fabric artwork decorates the far wall. Apollo makes for a great combined food and art outing, as the gallery is also well worth a visit.

Other than breakfast and sublime small plate dishes, from Tuesday to Friday the bar serves a simple but delicious and affordable daily lunch dish, such as chickpea salad or tomato soup, popular with art students. You can eat outside in the ivy-clad courtyard on warmer days, which is also the location of their summer parties.

Come the evening, there's usually cool music coming out of the speakers; and it's an ideal spot to mingle with a mixed crowd of gallerists, students and artists. The classical name is reflected in a plastercast statue and a Roman bust, plus an urn filled with fresh flowers. It's laidback, secluded and lovely.

Nyhavn 2

Kongens Nytorv

Tues 8am–5pm
Wed–Fri 8am–12am
Sat 10am–12am
Sun 10am–5pm

DKK
80–120

W
apollobar.dk

Smørrebrød + more

Fru Nimb

*Sample smørrebrød at this
elegant, long-established
spot in Tivoli.*

Bernstorffsgade, 1577
København V
88 70 00 00

København H

Mon–Sun 12pm–10pm

DKK
95–225

W
nimb.dk/en

Tivoli Gardens (see p.101) isn't exactly
Copenhagen's best-kept secret – it's a place
to find your inner kid amongst the nostalgic
o rides, pleasure gardens and Chinese
pagodas – but what's less obvious is that it
has some great eating options.

I love wandering the flower gardens
at Tivoli and then settling down indoors for
brunch or dinner at a white-linen covered
table at Fru Nimb (Mrs Nimb) for traditional
smørrebrød. Prettily arranged on the plate,
the sandwiches feature herring, roe and
smoked salmon, with garnishes of shaved
horseradish and feathery dill. Offerings
for meat lovers include steak tartare with
pickles, capers and horseradish, and smoked
pork with Russian salad and asparagus.

While the food is old-school with
a twist, the decor is harmoniously modern,
with white walls and crockery and
wooden Scandi-cool furniture. Fru Nimb
is a quintessential laidback Copenhagen
brunch spot. It's also fun to watch the Tivoli
illuminations and then enjoy dinner here.

Tivoli Food Hall

Snack on global food and watch the wonderful world of Tivoli.

Bernstorffsgade 3

33 15 10 01

København H

Sun–Thurs 11am–11pm

Fri & Sat 11am–12am

DKK

12–25

W

tivoligardens.com

This food hall enjoys a fabulous location, sitting at the north-western edge of Tivoli (see p.101), and allows you to see right into the famous amusement park, especially from the plant-wreathed upstairs viewing platform. If you're dithering about whether Tivoli is worth the admission fee (it is!), then go and grab a bowl of noodles here and check it out.

There's a wide range of options for diners, including organic spit-roasted chicken from Chicks by Chicks, authentic Italian pizza from Gorms and, of course, smørrebrød from Hallernes. There are plenty of vegetarian and gluten-free options available, including colourful salads from Icelandic chain Glo and Asian fusion food from Kung Fu Street Food which takes inspiration from Japan's traditional izakaya bars.

Smørrebrød + more

Told & Snaps

Lunch with the locals at this smart little smørrebrød spot.

Toldbodgade 2

33 93 83 85

Kongens Nytorv

Mon–Sun 11.30am–3.30pm

DKK

80–160

W

toldogsnaps.dk

This wee lunchtime spot near Amalienborg Palace is an utterly classic place to enjoy old-fashioned smørrebrød. It's tiny – you sit at white-linen draped tables in close proximity to fellow diners, who are mostly local business folk and retirees, while black and white photos of Danish monarchs gaze down on you. The shelves are lined with intriguing jars of their home-brewed snaps, looking like some crazy colourful lab experiment, with flavours including brown butter, licorice and raspberry.

You can choose from five varieties of herring smørrebrød alone, plus other fish and meat options. In fact, there's really nothing else on the menu, other than a couple of sweet choices.

Slurp Ramen

Big bowls of ramen with big flavours.

Nansensgade 90

53 70 80 83

Nørreport

Tues 12pm–2.30pm
Wed–Sun 12pm–2.30pm
& 5–10pm

DKK

140

W

slurpramen.dk

Slurp's the word here: the menu is short and to the point, with deep bowls of utterly delicious ramen. This smart little joint was set up by chef Philipp who stands in the open kitchen chopping, stirring and serving. Start with kimchi or a plate of edamame and horseradish, then move onto ramen. The umami flavours of the vegetable ramen are incredibly dense, with seasonal ingredients that might include oyster and portobello mushrooms, argula and lemon thyme. The Japanese philosophy they subscribe to here is tenrakai, which means improving every element, resulting in a kind of foodie nirvana.

With bar-stool seating and an efficient breezy air, it doesn't feel like a place to linger, but this fits with the Slurp theme: ramen starts losing its flavour if it's left to linger too long.

Smørrebrød + more

Selma

Get a Swedish take on Danish classics
at this beautiful backstreet fine-dining restaurant.

This restaurant is very much a personal project for chef Magnus Petersen –
it is even named after his daughter – and everything has been chosen
with love and care, from the lush Garden of Eden wallpaper to the wild
apple cider and Mikkeller craft brews. In fact, there's a dedication to craft
throughout: you'll dine from subtly colourful ceramic plates, while sitting on
an elegant bentwood chair and gazing at dainty 1930s glass vases, which
hold the flowers on each table. Rather than taking a minimalist Scandinavian
approach, this is a place of colour: signature warm yellow, plus eye-popping
fuchsia pink and tangerine toilets, inspired by Magnus's travels to India.

Crucially, Magnus is Swedish, and he feels his outsider view of Danish
smørrebrød has allowed him to reimagine classic dishes. He has taken trad
recipes – some of which have changed little in 150 years – and (respectfully)
shaken them up. His Christiansøpigens herring with brown butter, chives
and horseradish, for example, is scattered with rye bread crumble, rather than
served up in the usual open-sandwich style, while pan-fried scallops might
come with pickled pumpkin, ceps mushrooms or brussels sprouts, depending
on the season. Ingredients are entirely seasonal and the recipes are designed
on the basis of which are the best vegetables available. You can order a single
smørrebrød dish or go for the curated taster menu, which are all at very
reasonable prices.

📍		**DKK**
Rømersgade 20	Mon–Tues & Sun	100–145
93 10 72 03	11.30am–5pm	
	Wed–Sat 11.30am–12am	**W**
		selmacopenhagen.dk
Nørreport		

Smørrebrød + more

Vækst

This is my favourite Copenhagen restaurant in winter, when the light is low and you need greenery and light to brighten your mood.

The designers of Vækst have miraculously inserted a whole antique greenhouse into the restaurant: it sits over the steps leading down to the basement and floods the downstairs with light. The structure is densely hung with plants, giving it an exuberant tropical-hygge vibe. The furniture and floors are made from wood and small lights twinkle throughout, creating something of a magical forest-glade feeling.

Dishes at Vaekst are inspired by fresh Nordic vegetables and herbs, which are matched with fish and meat: they are big on scallops and beef tenderloin. There's a dedicated three-course 'green' menu for vegetarians, with mains such as grilled celeriac with fermented shiitake mushrooms, lovage and ransom capers. Everything is beautifully presented, including the dainty palate cleaners between each course and the sorbets which perfectly round off your meal, in flavours such as pear with roasted hazelnut and cherry with white chocolate and tonga bean.

Sankt Peders Stræde 34

38 41 27 27

Mon–Sun 12pm–2.45pm
& 5.30pm–12am

DKK

185–275

W

cofoco.dk

Vesterport

Smørrebrød + more

Barr

*Seasonal flavours and northern cuisine in a historic
harbourside warehouse.*

The mighty warehouse known as North Atlantic House (see p.145) is where
the culinary legend that is Noma first started. Noma has a more rustic
location in the city, and Barr, who is in the same restaurant group, resides
in its place, offering quality, seasonal food with a more casual atmosphere.
Barr's inspiration, both visually and in terms of flavours, comes from the
North and Baltic seas.

This handsome place has a harmonious interior, with wooden furniture
and floors and the heavy beams of the 17th-century warehouse overhead.
Seasonal flowers decorate the tables and there's a sense of the outside
coming in: the harbour water laps right outside and the restaurant is circled
by a northern garden featuring volcanic rocks and harebells.

Owner and chef Thorsten Schmidt is interested in exploring the
German and Danish food of his childhood and in transforming classic homely
northern dishes. Try the bone marrow waffles with luminous orange bleak roe,
sour cream and citrus herbs, or the delightfully colourful beetroot salad with
salted gooseberries and green strawberries. Desserts include a disc-shaped
sweet cake with sunflower seeds, white chocolate and blackcurrants. Barr
creates an impressive and ever-changing range of craft beers, including
earthy sour brews made with bacteria fermentation, honey and spiced mead,
smoked malt beer and pale ales.

Strandgade 93

32 96 32 93

Kongens Nytorv /
Christianshavn

Mon–Thurs 5–9.30pm

Fri–Sun 12pm–2pm &

5–9.30pm

DKK

155–260

W

restaurantbarr.com

Smørrebrød + more

Toldbod Bodega

Old-fashioned, irresistible Denmark in the oldest restaurant in the city.

Esplanaden 4

33 12 93 31

Marmorkirken

Tues–Sat 12pm–9pm

Sun 12pm–5pm

DKK

200

W

toldbod-bodega.dk

Stepping inside this back-in-time restaurant under the black awning is like walking into a painting; this is said to be the oldest restaurant in the city. If you like your hygge old-fashioned, warm-hearted and local, then this is the spot for you. The gilded outside sign is wreathed with images of grape vines, bright glass lanterns hang over the tables and framed portraits adorn the walls. It's gorgeous, slightly kitsch and very Danish.

Locals come in droves for the all-you-can-eat Tuesday supper of fried pork belly, potatoes, and parsley cream sauce. There's also herring galore, smoked eel and tasty crayfish salad, but what this place does best is cater for the Danish penchant for meat. Everything is, of course, washed down with a glass of aquavit.

Parterre

A welcoming, calming cafe for contemplation or a catchup with a friend.

Overgaden Oven Vandet 90

Christianshavn

Mon–Fri 7.30am–6pm
Sat & Sun 8am–6pm

DKK
100 breakfast plate

W

parterrechristianshavn.dk

For me, Parterre is the quintessential corner cafe: it isn't trying to do anything too fancy but what it does it does really well. It's located in Christianshavn, looks onto a canal and has a lovely cobbled backstreet vibe. Visit in the morning and you're likely to be knocked out by the sweet scent of cinnamon buns.

My favourite order is the highly photogenic breakfast plate consisting of a croissant, rye bread, a boiled egg, cheese, avocado and yoghurt with granola, compote and fresh berries. For lunch there's a simple sandwich menu. Throughout the day it's a great place to order a coffee; they do soy and oat milk, which can be a little hard to find elsewhere.

Smørrebrød + more

Bridge Street Kitchen

Al fresco eating at a street market with a harbour view.

I have to confess that I have eaten my way round this street market. I once lived nearby and the affordable and healthy eats, combined with a lively vibe and a pretty location on the harbour made it impossible to resist. As you sit and eat you can gaze at Operaen (The Royal Opera, see p.147), and watch the crowds build up at the little swing bridge, which stops the traffic when it opens to allow tall-masted ships to sail by.

In the summer months, try the super-healthy bowls and salads from California Kitchen, and a lime ice-cream from the nearby cart. Haddocks does British fish and chips, complete with mushy peas. Dhaba serves lamb and vegetable curries on edible plates and Danish classics are provided by Palægade. My own personal favourite is Mak-Cik, who rustle up Malaysian and Singaporean street food, including fantastic tofu bao with kimchi on the side and Malaysian lime lemonade to wash it down.

Strandgade 95
33 93 07 60

Nørreport

Mon–Sun 9am–late
(Apr–Oct)

DKK
95

W
thebridgestreetkitchen.com

Smørrebrød + more

Amass

Seasonal, stylish and sensational food.

There are now so many transformed industrial spaces and places on Refshaleøen but Amass was the pioneer in the area. It has been around since 2013 and still has a fresh and innovative approach. The restaurant is located in what was once the tool shed for the B&W shipping company – now a wide open space with graffiti decor that they recommission every year.

There's an open kitchen where the chefs use super-seasonal and homegrown ingredients to concoct some of the best food I've ever tasted. Last time I was there, they dished up what looked like just a bowl of summery cherry tomatoes, but they were dunked in smoked tomato oil and sprinkled with lemon basil and had a sweetly complex flavour and yielding texture that was simply mind-blowing. Other menu offerings might include grilled duck with bread miso, or chewy beetroots with walnut pulp custard and salted blackberries. For afters, try dark chocolate with beer grains and potato skin fudge.

Outside, Amass' beautiful vegetable and herb garden rises out of the semi-abandoned industrial landscape in simple wooden box frames and crates. There's nothing try-hard about the place, but it's a culinary and visual treat.

Refshalevej 153

43 58 43 30

2A

Tues–Fri 6pm–12am

Sat 12pm–3.30pm &
6pm–12am

DKK

1095 dinner menu

495 lunch menu

W

amassrestaurant.com

Smørrebrød + more

Reffen

Innovative global food in an industrial hipster haven.

Refshalevej 167

9A

Sun–Thurs 12pm–8pm
Fri–Sat 12pm–9pm
(Apr–Oct)

DKK
75–210

W
reffen.dk/en

I like to cycle to Refshaleøen on weekends, where young Copenhageners flock to socialise, inevitably winding up at Reffen, a salivatingly great market. Vendors operate from brightly painted shipping containers and shiny aluminium food vans and it is all about innovation – new food entrepreneurs are given space for three years to trial and develop their business.

You can eat your way round the world: Baobab cooks up Gambian peanut stews with fresh herbs and chilli mango on the side; Blue Taco create – yes – blue tacos made with blue corn; Everest serve lentil soup, steamed dumplings and other Nepalese delights; Kaburi Sushi is fresh and stylishly presented; while S'morebread gives the Danish open sandwich a lovely twist, loading bread with fresh herbs and edible flowers. Reffen's self-styled Village organises plenty of events to work off your lunch, including drop-in yoga, salsa classes and DJ events with dancing, plus there are quiz nights and concerts.

Hyggestund

Modernism-meets-hygge at this breakfast-fixated diner.

This Mikkeller-owned all-day breakfast cafe brings hygge style right up to date. It has a wonderful interior, where the walls and woodwork are painted in a warm colour that hovers between rust and peach. Candles and dried wildflowers decorate each of the intimately small tables, little lamps hang low and paintings and plants bring things to life.

Food inspiration comes from the all-American diner; they serve homemade waffles, doughnuts and ice-cream, spicy fried chicken, yoghurt bowls and avocado toast, washed down with organic sodas and juices, plus filter coffee and tea. Of course, Hyggestund also serve Mikkeller beers (see p.77), including the Beer Geek Breakfast coffee stout.

The name – Hyggestund – translates as a moment of hygge, and indeed it is!

Viktoriagade 6

31 61 55 19

København H

Mon–Thurs & Sun
9am–4.30pm
Fri & Sat 9am–11pm

DKK

94–179

W

hyggestund.dk

Smørrebrød + more

Plant Power Food

Bright, bold and super-healthy vegan food.

Plant Power Food is a relative newcomer to the city's foodie scene, started by a former professional handball player Caspar and his chef partner Neel, both of whom are passionate about intensely healthy food that rely on techniques other than frying. Marinating and dehydrating of ingredients are key approaches, resulting in some intense flavours. There's a focus on raw food and all the dishes are colourful, bountiful, imaginative and utterly delicious. Last time I ate here, a neighbouring diner exclaimed: 'this is a party on a plate!' And it really is.

It's an intimate place with plain furnishings, white walls and exuberant plants, allowing the food to be the star. They serve up warm dishes, such as chipotle with rice and quinoa, imaginative tapas including king trumpet ceviche with truffle caviar and (surprisingly yummy) black cracker dust, and beautifully wrapped rice paper rolls drizzled with tahini. You can eat gluten-free smørrebrød here, and the sole dessert – sweet potato truffles in dark chocolate – is the bomb. There's an excellent line in non-alcoholic gin and rum cocktails which offer good times without the hangover, as well as the lip-smacking cranberry dream mocktail made from cranberry juice, kombucha with raspberries, cranberries and fresh mint.

9
Fælledvej 15
93 30 66 15

Nørrebros Runddel St
5C

⊙
Mon–Sun 10am–10pm

DKK
128–185

W
plantpowerfood.dk

Smørrebrød + more

Andersen & Maillard

Barista coffee and pastries to die for.

Nørrebrogade 62

42 67 21 00

Nørrebros Runddel

5C

Mon–Sun 7am–7pm

DKK

350

W

andersenmaillard.dk

There are lots of spots in town to get great coffee but where Andersen & Maillard excel is with their baking, concocted by a former Noma and Amass (see p.51) chef. The deconstructed pain au chocolat is a winner: a complex muffin-shaped twirl of chocolate and flaky pastry that dissolves in the mouth. Other superb innovations include espresso-glazed croissants and a half croissant turned into a cone for homemade espresso ice-cream. They do their coffee right, too. There's an in-house roastery so the beans are super-fresh and baristas can provide a caffeine fix any way you like – complete with delicate latte art.

Decor is light, bright and funky, with picture windows providing perfect Nørrebro people-watching opportunities. You'll see some interesting coffee-related objects on sale too, such as dainty metal kettles, drippers and own-brand coffee.

Manfreds

*Fresh farm-to-table food
on a destination street.*

Jægersborggade 40

36 96 65 93

Nørrebros Runddel

Mon–Sun 12pm–3.30pm
& 5–10pm

DKK

Plates 90

Chef's choice menu 195

W

manfreds.dk/en

Manfreds sits on my favourite shopping street in Copenhagen: lively and inventive Jægersborggade (see p.173). You can sit outside and check out the strolling hipster locals or eat inside in the homely bistro-style interior, where plates are charmingly mismatched and sustainability rather than Scandi cool is the key note.

Farm-to-table food is the philosophy here, with produce coming from their organic growing space at Svanholm. There are à la carte choices, and it's famous for its steak tartare, but the chef's choice menu is entirely guided by the seasonal and sustainable bounty of the farm. The idea is to share small plates of goodies, such as celeriac with salted perch, pike and quinoa, or roasted pumpkin with elderflower and smoked yolk. The food is 90–100 percent organic and the wines are natural.

Smørrebrød + more

Souls

*Plant-based soul food, combining Australian
and Danish creativity.*

This is the first of what has become a small Copenhagen chain, with the informal, yet intensely foodie, Australian vibe of the co-founders fusing beautifully with the chef's Danish aesthetic. Souls' bare brick and white walls, and reclaimed timber tables are attractive but it's the plant-based food that literally shines, from lime green smoothies to the lychees and blueberries embedded in thick cashew yoghurt and rainbow plates of fruit. The weekend brunch is a cornucopia of healthy food, served on long dishes lined with little pots of sweet and savoury goodness. There's scrambled tofu, pulled portobello mushrooms with smoked eggplant (which tastes ridiculously meaty), overnight oats with a hint of lavender, homemade jam with pear and rosehip (sweetened with agave not sugar), and piles of American-style pancakes.

For lunch and dinner, the big hit is the 'beyond meat' burgers, including a king oyster mushroom version lavished with their own barbecue sauce that's to die for. Chilli bowls are warm with soy mince, beans and peas, red pepper, tomato, herbs, quinoa and tempura 'parmesan' chips. And drinks are super-imaginative: try the iced-coconut latte or the Aussie lemonade with mango, eucalyptus and lemon.

Melchiors Plads. 3
34 10 01 01

Trianglen

Mon–Wed 10am–9.30pm
Thurs & Fri 10am–10pm
Sat 9am–10pm
Sun 9am–8.30pm

DKK
Brunch 134
Burgers 110

W
soulscph.dk

Smørrebrød + more

Juno the Bakery

*The best cardamom
buns in the city, bar none.*

Århusgade 48

Trianglen

Wed–Sat 7.30am–6pm
Sun 8am–3pm

DKK

24

This little bakery is scarcely more than a hole in the wall – there's a servery, a few tables inside and out, and space for the bakers to knead, cut and bake thick piles of dough. It's a bit out of the way, but if you want to explore Danish baking it's really worth hopping on your bike to come over here for the almond croissants, sourdough buns with comté cheese and ... everyone's favourite, the amazing kardemommeboller (cardamom buns). These little beauties are a figure-of-eight tangle of soft pastry, dotted with seed pods, topped with sugar crystals and gently browned. Irresistible.

Once you've sampled these, have a taste of Juno's Kanelgifler cinnamon: moist pastry parcels containing brown sugar, cinnamon and salted butter. In blackberry season, go for the roasted hazelnut frangipane tarts topped with plump fruits; the elongated rhubarb tarts with vanilla cream, framed by croissant pastry, are also scrumptious.

Alouette

A serious foodie's fine-dining destination.

Sturlasgade 14P
3167 6606

Islands Brygge

Thurs–Sat 5.15pm–12am

DKK
Menu 795

W
restaurant-alouette.dk

Approaching Alouette across a scruffy courtyard, you'd be forgiven for thinking you'd lost your way entirely. The restaurant is set in an old 1920s envelope factory, whose rooms are now used for band practice. You ascend in a graffitied goods elevator and emerge into a glamourously revamped space that's a world away from the surroundings, with pale colours, tasteful furnishings gleaming with bronze and a vine looping across the ceiling.

This is very much a foodie destination, where you have to reserve a table in advance. The kitchen is wide open, and much of the cooking is done on an open fire. A signature dish is turbot cooked in bone sauce, but the menu changes constantly with the seasons. Each serving consists of five courses of carefully considered food; you might encounter king crab, truffles, Norwegian scallops, Danish squid and all manner of other good things.

HYGGE DRINKS + NIGHTLIFE

The Danes like a drink – this is the country of Carlsberg after all – and more recently the country of impeccably hip craft breweries, such as Broaden & Build (see p.73) and Mikkeller Baghaven (see p.72). Local offerings include spirits, super-strong aquavit, snaps and festive Christmas gløgg (mulled wine), which usually throws flaked almonds, raisins and cinnamon into the delicious mulled wine mix. Or opt for on-trend natural wines at Pompette (see p.82) and several other venues around town. The drinking scene in the city is very convivial and mixes upbeat boozy hedonism with a strong shot of hygge. Outdoor venues have piles of blankets to wrap up in, candles and lanterns light the pubs on winter nights, and visitors are generally welcomed at bars with genuine warmth.

If you're looking for nightlife, there are plenty of options, from jazz at classic venue Jazzclub (see p.69) to organ concerts in Vor Frelsers Kirke (Our Saviour's Church, see p.71). You might like to party onboard an old ferry at Kontiki (see p.70) or catch a movie and play a board game at Huset (see p.65).

Huset

From board games and gigs to classic
movies and hearty food.

Founded way back in 1970 and housed in rambling, impossibly charismatic 15th- and 18th-century buildings, this self-styled culture house is a one-stop shop for a night on the tiles. Buzzy and unstuffy, it packs unbelievable numbers into the downstairs board game cafe and bar (called, inexplicably, Bastard Café), where analogue fun-seekers have a choice of over 2000 games. Huset's youthful energy makes it pretty irresistible, and it's a warm and welcoming place for solo travellers – if you're in need of a fun and sociable night out, then this is the spot.

There's an attractive courtyard bar area, strung with coloured lights, and at the affordable bistro-style restaurant you can sit at trestle tables under wooden beams and eat tasty vegan pizza or salmon served with roe and black rice.

Music venue Musikcaféen on the third floor hosts gigs, stand-up and storytelling nights, while a kitschly kitted out cinema – Husets Biograf – programmes film noir classics, Scandi classics and cult movies, which you can watch curled up in an armchair. They excel at interactive movie nights, teaming themed drinks and eats with cinematic singalongs.

Rådhusstræde 13
Bastard Café
42 74 66 42
Hussets Biograf
20 29 70 13

Mon–Thurs & Sun
12pm–12am
Fri–Sat 12pm–2am
Bastard Fri 12pm–2am

huset-kbh.dk

Kongens Nytorv

Hygge drinks + nightlife

Cinemateket

Experimental movies screened in a modern theatre.

Gothersgade 55

33 74 34 12

Nørreport

Mon–Sun 10am–11pm

W

dfi.dk

Anyone like me who loves arthouse cinema will love Cinemateket. It's the cinema of the Danish Film Institute, and is housed in a handsome modern film theatre programming interesting new releases, documentaries and one-off favourites. There are three screens, and it's worth dropping in at any time of day to catch a classic. They screen a lot of English-language movies.

Cinemateket sits opposite the green space of Kongens Have, and it has a decent cafe–bar where you can sit at the picture windows and watch people passing by. They dish up sandwiches, snacks, pastries and hot and cold drinks.

Palæ Bar

*Have a boozy night
out with the locals at this
side-street bar.*

Ny Adelgade 5

33 12 54 71

Kongens Nytorv

Mon–Wed 11am–1am
Thurs–Sat 11am–3am
Sun 4pm–1am

W
palaebar.dk

There's something gorgeously old-fashioned about Palæ Bar – it feels to me like stepping into a bar in Left Bank Paris circa 1920s, and partying with intellectual glitterati. You might meet journalists, artists, politicians, writers or party animals, and there's always the feeling that anything might happen – from dancing on the tables to beer-fuelled romance.

Palæ sits on a back street near Kongens Nytorv square, its rust-red painted exterior identifiable by a neon-lit mermaid sipping from a saxophone. The warm hyggelige interior is hung with canvases, vintage metal advertising signs, saxophones and trumpets and a Michelin Man lamp. It hosts free jazz nights monthly on Sundays; see the website for dates.

Hygge drinks + nightlife

Balderdash

Wacky cocktails mixed in a 300-year old mansion.

Valkendorfsgade 11

Gammel Strand /
Kongens Nytorv

Wed–Sat 5pm–3am

W

balderdash.dk

Balderdash is a place where everyone knows your name, and, if they don't, they'll find it out pretty quickly and yell it over the bar at you. The welcome is high-energy and the vibe fun, with cocktail shakers being spun through the air. And they are properly imaginative about their drinks here. A peek at the drinks list reveals some wildly arcane options, such as the Lost cocktail, with empirical pasilla distillate, mushroom–maple switchel and banana and black walnut. While the jury is out on what some of these ingredients are, the combination is sure to be fabulous.

This is one of the city centre's oldest buildings – it dates back to 1732 – and was renovated in a quirkily appealing style by the bar's owner, Geoffrey. The timbered interior has some serious nooks and crannies, and the glass shelves of the bar are crammed with bottles of esoteric spirits.

Jazzclub

*An old-time jazz club
deep in leafy Christiania.*

Psyak off Pusher Street

Christianshavn

Mon–Sun 7pm–late

Copenhagen has had a long and loving relationship with jazz; several African-American star musicians, such as Ben Wester, came to the city in the 1960s and '70s, and ended up making it their home. Jazzclub, which sits right in the centre of Christiania, has been around since 1998; it grew out of Christiania's wind ensemble and the leading figure behind it was Jes Harpsøe. This is a wonderfully earthy place to hear live improvisational music every Wednesday and Friday night. While many of the city's other venues go for the dinner-jazz vibe and charge a fortune for entry, Jazzclub is affordable and welcoming.

The stage is hung with canvases and guitars and prettily lit with coloured lights, making it one of the city's most attractive venues – in a low-key way. Emerging into the lantern-strung but otherwise dark streets of night-time Christiania is all part of the magic.

Kontiki

Party on the harbour on this former ferry turned super-fun bar.

Takkelloftvej 1z

40 50 90 48

2A

Mon–Sun 11am–9pm

W

kontikibar.dk

This bar on a boat is a blast, a party spot moored just across from the Operaen (The Royal Opera, see p.147); the family who owns the boat grew up on board, and it's run with love. The vessel dates back to 1933, it was once an island ferry and the restoration has preserved its rugged character. There are three levels inside and a cute wooden bar on deck, and they have an impressive list of organic, sulphate-free natural wines, most of them Italian.

One wacky feature is the glass-bottomed toilets, where you can see harbour fish swimming below your feet and, if you're unlucky, one of the students from the nearby college buildings – who allegedly have some summer fun by swimming under the boat.

Vor Freslers Kirke (Our Saviour's Church)

Organ concerts in a landmark Christianshavn church.

Sankt Annæ Gade 29

32 54 68 83

Christianshavn

Mon–Sun 11am–9pm

W

vorfrelserskirke.dk

The distinctive corkscrew spire of Our Saviour's Church soars some 90 metres (300 feet) above Christianshavn. By day you can climb its 400 steps for a bird's-eye perspective of the island, but I love visiting in the evening, when the lights dim and the stunning wooden organ is used for free recitals.

Dominating the barn-like interior, the organ was built from 1696–98 and is the largest, oldest and best example of a German organ anywhere. It is supported on the wall by two sculpted elephants (the symbol of absolute monarchy) and has more than 4000 pipes. Check the website to find out about concerts, which are programmed around four times per month.

Hygge drinks + nightlife

Mikkeller Baghaven

Hip Refshaleøen at its experimental best.

Refshalevej 169B

22 89 85 32

2A

Mon–Thurs & Sun 12pm–10pm
Fri & Sat 12pm–12am

W

mikkeller.com

Follow the signs from Reffen (see p.52) to find the giant former shipbuilding yard that houses Baghaven. It's a super-sociable and relaxed spot on a summer day: you can sit at the benches outside and nurse your craft beer at the harbour's edge. The place is part-brewery, part-science lab, with rustic farmhouse ales, as well as wild ales concocted with introduced yeast. They excel in alternative fermentation, using foraged yeast and bacteria. In the tasting room you sit under large oak barrels, where the brews are aged – some of them in soft fruits. The ales are produced in limited numbers, making this a really interesting and bespoke drinking experience for beer fans.

A simple menu of food helps to soak up the booze: Baghaven dish up flatbreads, fried chicken and charcuterie, as well as snacks such as fried shrimp, smoked nuts and beef jerky.

Broaden & Build

Industrial chic, artisan beer and fantastic food.

Refshalevej 175A

73 70 81 70

2A

Wed & Thurs 3–10pm
Fri & Sat 12pm–11pm
Sun 12pm–7pm

broadenbuildcph.com

Run by the team behind ace restaurant Amass (see p.51), Broaden & Build was always going to be a winner. It's a dramatic, hugely high-ceilinged brewery bar located near the Contemporary Copenhagen gallery (see p.150). The exterior is weathered concrete, with a stylish neon sign hung on the battered industrial shutters. Inside there are bold and bright geometric murals, and the shiny vats and pipes of the brewery are all part of the show.

Expert bar staff advise drinkers sitting at the long bar on the amazing range of home brews, which contain Scandi seasonal ingredients such as sea buckthorn, rhubarb, blackened pears, fennel and elderflower. As you'd expect from Amass's sister business, the food here is fantastic, some of it beer-inspired, such as the spiced grain crisps and fried fermented potatoes.

Hygge drinks + nightlife

Lidkoeb

*A historic former apothecary housing one
of the city's most stylish and cosy bars.*

This cocktail bar tucked away in an 18th-century building in a Vesterbro
backyard manages to combine two essential but seemingly contradictory
Scandinavian elements: hygge and modish minimalist design. The hygge bit
consists of warming fur rugs, a piano, an ancient wood-beamed open fire and
a huge collection of malt whiskies: the whole top floor is devoted to a whisky
bar, with over 200 varieties. Here under the attic eaves, the owners are
keen to cultivate a communal sitting room vibe. They ask that you don't take
photos or talk on your phone, but rather sink into a Chesterfield armchair to
savour a single malt or a whisky cocktail and some conversation. Downstairs
you can sip a banana and walnut daiquiri or a pear swizzle with bourbon.
The city's famous design credentials are reflected in the muted colour palette,
1950s original Børge Mogensen wood and leather chairs and long copper-
topped bar.

More than anything though, I've found that Lidkoeb is a place to
do what the Danes do best of all: have fun. In summer the courtyard is
thronged with drinkers, and all year round expertly made cocktails keep
the party spirit alive.

Vesterbrogade 72B

33 11 20 10

Enghave Plads

Mon–Tues & Sun

8pm–2am

Wed–Sat 4pm–2am

W

lidkoeb.dk

Hygge drinks + nightlife

Dyrehaven

An old-school bar given a hip makeover.

Sønder Blvd 72

33 21 60 24

Enghave Plads

Mon–Sat 9.30am–2am

Sun 9.30am–10pm

W

dyrehavenkbh.dk

Cool little Dyrehaven cafe and bar in Vesterbro sits just off Sønder Boulevard, and is identifiable by the deer's head logo on the windows. Antlers are hung on the deep blue walls inside, where orange metal pendant lights and slatted wooden benches tucked into booths make for a traditional interior. The original bar here was 100 years old and the new owners have sought to preserve something of its comforting vibe.

Dyrehaven has a very European feel, serving up barista coffee and big breakfasts in the morning, sandwich and salad lunches, and then moving into the evening with bistro dishes such as ragout and saltimbocca. It has a huge range of bottled and draught beers, from oatmeal pale ales to sour shandies and pilsners, with American and Belgian brews, as well as local ones. The wine list is comprised of organic and natural vintages, including an orange Austrian tipple.

Mikkeller Viktoriagade

An inventive microbrewery using experimental brewing techniques.

Viktoriagade 8 B-C

33 31 04 15

København H

Mon–Wed & Sun 1pm–1am
Thurs & Fri 1pm–1am
Sat 1pm–2am

W
mikkeller.com

Mikkeller is a ubiquitous presence on the city's drinking scene. This is one of their most appealing outlets, and does what Copenhagen does best: injecting a dose of imagination and creative style into a beautiful old building.

The bar sits in the cellar basement of an ornately sculpted 19th-century mansion and is decked out with simply chic minimalist stools and quirkily mismatched chairs. Little cabinets are hung on the walls, providing a place to place your craft ale. It serves twenty changing taps from its own brewery and around the world, which come in bespoke glasses or bottles with bright cartoonish labels. There are gluten-free and non-alcoholic brews on offer too, and snacks such as Danish cheeses and handmade sausages. In summer, the cellar doors open wide and drinkers congregate at the tables and benches outside.

Hygge drinks + nightlife

Blågårdsgade nightlife

*Roam this lively street at night to find
your new favourite bar.*

If you'd like a night out, take a stroll down Blågårdsgade, where you'll find the liveliest bars and cafes in town. There's a palpable convivial buzz here: the street is packed with hundreds of bicycles, parked up as their owners party, chat, drink and generally make merry.

My favourite venue here is corner cafe Blågårds Apotek (Blågårds Plads 2), a converted pharmacy, now a non-profit space hosting jams, gigs and exhibitions. For great bars, try little Harbo Bar (no.2) for organic Danish beer, charming Props for beer and coffee (no.5) and trendy chic wine bar Vinhanen (no.13). If you're peckish, you can tuck into vegetarian curries, stir fries and stews at funky Kate's Joint (no.12), dumplings at Gao (no.3) and Mexican food at Blue Taco (no.1).

But it's the street itself that is the star, its trestle tables thronged with party people. If you are looking to make new friends in Copenhagen, this is a great place to start.

Blågårdsgade

Hours vary

W
lidkoeb.dk

Nørreport / Forum /
Nørrebros Runddel

5C

Hygge drinks + nightlife

Alice

The best spot for interesting gigs in the city.

This experimental music venue is located in a little courtyard up an alley off Nørre Allé. It can be a little hard to spot, but if you're a music fan it's well worth seeking out. The mid-sized auditorium with a simple bar has hosted some of the greats and must-sees of modern music, including the San Ra Arkestra. The venue is named for genius composer, jazz singer, pianist and harpist Alice Coltrane – wife of John Coltrane.

Last time I went to Alice there was a trio blasting the room with avant garde sound, the saxophonist blowing her soprano sax straight into the microphone; the evening exemplified this venue's approach to challenging progressive music.

The programming is thoughtful and it's worth taking a punt on whoever is playing here, whether you're into jazz, roots, improv, electronica or sonic experiments.

Nørre Allé 7
50 58 08 41

Hours vary

alicecph.com

Nørrebros Runddel

Hygge drinks + nightlife

Pompette

A chic Parisian-style bar, specialising in natural wines.

Møllegade 3

Nørrebros Runddel

Mon–Thurs 2pm–12am
Fri–Sun 12pm–12am

W

pompette.dk

Natural wine is a big craze in Copenhagen, and this petite French wine bar is the best spot to sample it. Pompette is located on Møllegade, just off the main street in Nørrebro, and is cleverly screened by greenery, creating a snug backstreet Paris-vibe. Bright wine bottles and plants line the window sills and the walls are artfully distressed; you can sample your vintage on a tall stool inside, or on warmer days opt for the bistro-style seats and little tables outside.

There's a simple system for wine quaffers: you simply order a glass of red, white, orange or rosé, any of which costs DKK 50, a bit of a bargain in this pricey town. The name means tipsy in French, which you might well be after a seductive evening here. Snack on their charcuterie and cheese, including an excellent burrata.

Yellow

Shake up your night with a cocktail at this cosy bar.

Kapelvej 1

46 92 23 82

Nørrebros Runddel

Mon–Wed 4pm–12am
Thurs 4pm–1am
Fri & Sat 12pm–3am

W
yellowkbh.dk

This small cocktail gastro bar is named for the distinctive yellow wall of the Assistens Cemetery (see p.131), which sits opposite. It's an unassuming place, with a tiled bar where bottles and copper cocktail shakers gleam.

The bar staff are expert in shaking up boozy delights using seasonal ingredients and high-quality spirits, and you can also down natural wines and Danish craft beers here. Snuggle up inside under the mural wall, or catch the vibes on the street outside while sipping your Naked and Famous (Aperol, mezcal, yellow chartreuse and lime). They serve oysters and shareable snacks, some with Japanese flavours. And DJ nights on Fridays are a late-night blast.

Hygge drinks + nightlife

Sidecar

*Cool cocktails, great
Asian food and Sunday
night jazz.*

Skyttegade 5

20 99 97 27

Nuuks Plads

Mon 8am–4pm

Tues & Wed 8am–10.30pm

Thurs 8am–12am

Fri 8am–12.30am

Sat 9.30am–12am

Sun 9.30am–10.30pm

W

sidecarnoerrebro.dk

Located in a residential area in deepest Nørrebro, Sidecar is a bit of a city secret. Look out for the blue walls and head inside to the glowing modern bar. It serves an array of imaginative cocktails, such as the Mezmintrising (Mezcal, creme de cassis, lime, gomme, egg white and mint) and the sensational Rosella (plum wine with vodka, bitters, hibiscus tea and chilli).

For food, former pop-up Maobao has popped up permanently at Sidecar in the evenings, dishing up dumplings, bao (steamed buns) and other fresh Asian dishes. Visit during the day and you can enjoy the epic brunch, piled up on a rustic table in the centre of the bar. On Sunday evenings this turns into one of the city's most intimate and fun venues, with a varied roster of avant-garde jazz bands.

Toldboden

*Harbour-front beers in
the old customs house.*

Nordre Toldbod 18–24

33 93 38 28

Marmorkirken

Mon–Thurs 11am–5pm
Fri 11am–11pm
Sat & Sun 9.30am–5pm

W

toldboden.com

I've never weathered a storm in this
harbourfront bar but I'm sure it'd be a lot
of fun. Toldboden is sited out near the spot
where The Little Mermaid (see p.115) sits,
and is housed in a low brick building – the
city's former customs house – with picture
windows looking right out onto the water.
There's a long list of cocktails, plus wines
and draft beers. Food is hearty: try the
lobster hotdog with shrimps, fries, pea dip
and greens.

Outside, there are sturdy tables
and benches and a sculpture composed
of characterfully rusting nautical dials and
cogs. Inside, the rugged tables are
made from reclaimed timber, thick ropes coil
up the columns, hyggelige sheepskin rugs
are thrown on the benches and fairy lights
twinkle on the fishing nets hung from the
ceiling. All you need now is a friendly storm.

Hygge drinks + nightlife

DR Koncerthuset (concert hall)

An exciting modern music venue.

Located in what are still the wilds of Amager, Koncerthuset is a remarkable building, seeming to rear up out of the grasses. Designed by French architect Jean Nouvel and opened in 2009, it has rather an unfinished vibe from the outside, looking a little as if it is wrapped in temporary blue cladding. These blue screens represent the nearby water and are used to best effect when lit up with projections.

Inside, there are four halls and a stunning if somewhat vertiginous auditorium seating 1800 people, its wooden tiers of seating rising high above the wide stage. With its excellent acoustics, this is the perfect foil for the resident Danish National Symphony Orchestra, as well as the Danish Radio Big Band. The main hall is dedicated to classical music, while there are jazz concerts in the foyer, and the three other spaces feature choral and electronic music, plus pop and rock gigs.

Koncerthuset's restaurant serves high-quality seasonal food, and its floor-to-ceiling windows provide sweeping views of this emerging district. Check the website for the musical program and reserve ahead for the restaurant.

Ørestads Blvd. 13

35 20 62 62

Hours vary

W

drkoncerthuset.dk

DR Byen

Hygge drinks + nightlife

DON'T MISS

Copenhagen is a relaxed and relaxing city and not a place where you'll be wanting to hurtle from sight to sight. That said, there are plenty of galleries, museums and palaces that are worth making a (leisurely) beeline for. Two of my personal favourites are Glypoteket (see p.95), with its art and botanic gardens, and the David Collection (see p.99) of Islamic and Danish art. For an insight into the much-loved royals, ogle the crown jewels or walk the beautiful gardens of Rosenborg Palace (see p.103) and the stately rooms of Christiansborg Palace (see p.97). For the big-hitters, take your time to view the vast collection of Statens Museum for Kunst (National Gallery of Denmark, see p.93), or dive into Viking history at Nationalmuseet (National Museum of Denmark, see p.105). Tivoli (see p.101) is so wildly popular as to be off-putting, but an evening date there is still one of the most romantic and magical experiences the city has to offer.

At every turn there are water views and varied architecture, so getting to your destination is half the fun, whether you opt for a cycle ride (see p.123) or a trip on one of the battered yellow harbour bus boats (see p.91).

The Harbour

*Hopping on some kind of boat
in Copenhagen is a must.*

Copenhagen is a maritime city, defined by its harbour, and one of the great ways to experience the place is on a boat. The most basic, cheapest and perhaps most characterful option is the tough old yellow harbour bus boats that chug up and down the harbour: you can even wheel your bike on. There are stops up and down the waterway, and you can buy tickets onboard.

This being Copenhagen, there are a couple of terrific eco options, too. You can self-drive a GoBoat (Islands Brygge 10, mid-March–Oct), which is particularly fun in a group – the little blue solar-powered vessels all have a raised picnic table for onboard wining and dining. The most adventurous option, GreenKayak (Børskaj 12, mid-March–Oct) will provide you with a kayak, plus a big bucket and rubbish grabber – set off with a pal or partner and help keep the harbour clean.

Another innovative local company is Hey Captain (Ofelia Plads, mid-March–mid-Dec), whose brilliantly informative skipper/guides wear jaunty nautical T-shirts and take you all round the harbour – and deep into Copenhagen's culture and history. Book in advance to ensure a place: the boats seat a maximum of 12 people, in a semi-circle to promote sociability. The vessels are open but can be covered if rain hits. Hey Captain's evening trips, when you can wrap up in a blanket and the boats are lit by lanterns, rate high on the hygge scale.

Various locations

Hours vary

W

goboat.dk
greenkayak.org
heycaptain.dk

Don't miss

Statens Museum for Kunst (National Gallery of Denmark)

The city's national gallery is a big beast, housed in a vast Neoclassical building.

Dive into this huge collection of European art, holding over a quarter of a million paintings and sculptures, drawings and prints, as well as plaster casts of Classical and Renaissance works. I confess to having taken a deep breath before first plunging into the vast late 19th-century gallery, and suggest that you tackle the gallery in stages or dip in for a taster from each display.

The main galleries circle around the first floor. Raoul Dufy's bright *Landscape near Vence* stopped me in my tracks in the sensual French Art collection, where there are also more works by Matisse than any gallery outside France. Munch's forceful *Workers Returning Home* in the more angst-ridden Danish and Nordic Art section is viscerally powerful. In the European Art section you can explore the Italian Renaissance, admire some still Dutch interiors and Rembrandt's craggy portraits, or come up to date with changing exhibitions and installation work.

The gallery is based on a royal collection and prides itself on its paintings from the Danish Golden Age (1800–50), when the country was in political and financial turmoil and a style of painting emerged that might be paradoxically termed Romantic Realism, with landscapes and urban scenes suffused with gentle northern light. Downstairs there's a light and stylish cafe, Kafeteria, as well as an excellent shop, with a particularly good line in children's mobiles.

📍	🕙	**DKK**
Sølvgade 48–50	Tues & Thurs–Sun 10am–6pm	100 (children are free)
🚌	Wed 10am–8pm	**W**
Nørreport		smk.dk/en

Don't miss

Glyptoteket

*Classical sculptures, Impressionist paintings
and an exotic winter garden.*

This art collection meets botanic garden meets elegant cafe is one of Copenhagen's most beautiful and enriching places. It's set in a flamboyant red brick building where a copper and glass dome shelters a wonderful winter garden, and abundant ferns and palm trees cluster round a pond. At the centre sits Kai Nielsen's ice white sculpture, *The Water Mother*, a naked woman surrounded by multiple suckling babies.

The original collection was gathered by Carl Jacobsen, son of the founder of the Carlsberg brewing empire. It concentrates on sculptures, with the first floor being devoted to the ancient world. In the Greek and Roman section, portrait heads glow against the strikingly bright coloured gallery walls. On the same floor is an outstanding display of Egyptian works, spanning 3000 years. One of the most remarkable objects is a 5000-year-old sculpture of a lively hippo, one foot raised. In complete contrast, in the upstairs gallery there's a small but dazzling gallery of French Impressionist paintings, with canvases by Monet, Pissarro, Gaugin, Cézanne, plus post-Impressionist masterpieces by Toulouse Lautrec and Van Gogh. Go up to the top floor and you'll find works by Rodin, and Degas' touching bronze dancers.

Picnic, the gallery's cafe, serves superb modern, seasonal dishes and the book and gift shop is full of covetable things. In summer, classical concerts are held in a temple-like auditorium.

Dantes Plads 7

Tues–Sun 11am–6pm

DKK

115, Tues free

København H /
Rådhuspladsen

W

glyptoteket.com

Don't miss

Christiansborg Palace

*Explore the royal palace where the city
of Copenhagen was born.*

Slotsholmen is a compact piece of land in the city centre, dominated by commanding Christiansborg Palace; it's where the country's parliament and supreme court sit. The palace's reception rooms are used by the Danish queen, Queen Margrethe, for official business. Despite the fabled informality and earthiness of the country's royalty, the palace rooms have a rather stultifying air, with endless gleaming columned rooms: the Throne Room is where the queen receives guests and the Velvet Room hosts banquets. However, things come to life in the Great Hall with the modern tapestry room: created in 2000, these woollen wonders track Danish history from the Vikings onwards, bringing things up to date with the fall of the Berlin Wall and the first moon landing.

Visitors can also explore the royal stables, chapel and kitchens, lined with huge copper pans. But below the ground is the most intriguing of Slotsholmen's structures: the remnants of the castle built by Bishop Absalon in the 12th century, which marked the foundation of the modern city. Here you can see the remains of the curtain wall that protected the city from pirates, as well as more recent fire-ravaged ruins, such as the blue tower, where poor Leonora Christina was imprisoned in the 17th century for 21 years for the treasonous crimes of her husband.

To see where the royals live or the changing of the guard, head to Amalienborg Castle.

📍	⏷	**DKK**
Prins Jørgens Gård 1	Tues–Sun 9am–5pm	160
	(Apr–Oct)	
🚌	Tues–Sun 10am–5pm	**W**
Gammel Strand	(Nov–Mar)	kongeligeslotte.dk

Don't miss

David Collection

*A glittering hoard of Islamic art treasures and
Danish paintings in a park-side mansion.*

My personal favourite house museum on a rainy day in Copenhagen is
the David Collection, amassed by lawyer Christian Ludvig David between
1910 and 1960. The house itself is a tall and handsome 1806 building facing
Rosenborg Palace (see p.103) across the park. The contents, which merit
a half day to explore, fall into three distinct parts. David's early modern
Danish art collection beautifully reflects the natural world and folk art of the
country, and includes delicate psychological portraits by Vilhelm Hammershøi.
The European Art collection focuses very much on decorative arts, such as
porcelain, faïence and fine furniture.

But it's the Islamic collection that literally dazzles here, from gleaming
silk textile fragments dating back to 8th century Damascus to
the diamond-studded bling of the Mughal Empire. Dimly lit rooms reveal
dainty miniatures, bold ceramics, scientific objects and weaponry, amounting
to an education in the entire history of Islam.

One of the most precious pieces is a dagger that is said to have
belonged to Tipu Sultan, the ruler of Mysore until his death at the hands of
the British in 1799. The double-edged dagger has a gold hilt and scabbard,
and is set with rows of diamonds, rubies and emeralds. Also mesmerising is a
14th-century gilded Chinese caftan, a delicate survivor from the middle ages.

⚲	⊙	DKK
Kronprinsessegade 30	Tues & Thurs–Sun	Free
	10am–5pm	
�	Wed 10am–9pm	W
Nørreport /		davidmus.dk
Marmokirken		

Don't miss

Tivoli

*Fairytale Denmark lives on at this
enchanting pleasure garden.*

The Danes have always had a penchant for amusement and escapism:
Tivoli is the second oldest amusement park in the world (the oldest also
being in Denmark: Dyrehavsbakken in Klampenborg). Perhaps at its most
magical in the evening, it's a place to utterly surrender to full-blown hygge
enjoyment, and to let your inner child come out to play. Tivoli has all the
stomach-churning rides you could ever want – or not as the case may be!
But it's also a beautiful park and pleasure garden, where artistry and
innovation have always been key elements, with a central lake, tall trees and
ingenious hanging planting. The geometric lights in the trees were created
by contemporary Icelandic artist Olafur Eliasson, and the Flying Trunk, an
undulating ride through Hans Christian Andersen's tales, uses folk artistry
to create a captivating experience. If you're seeking some thrills, the 1914
Rutschebanen is the oldest rollercoaster in the world, and the modern
Dæmonen (Demon) rollercoaster takes screaming participants through three
huge loops and drops in sixty seconds. Or you might prefer the more sedate
merry-go-rounds, featuring brightly painted sleighs and animals.

There are umpteen options for eating and drinking: Fru Nimb
(see p.36) does an elegant take on smørrebrød (open sandwiches), while
unpretentious Grøften and serves old-school smørrebrød and has changed
very little since its 19th-century founding. There is also a plethora of stalls
selling snacks and drinks

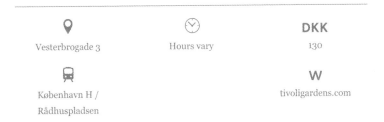

⊙	**⊙**	**DKK**
Vesterbrogade 3	Hours vary	130
🚌		**W**
København H /		tivoligardens.com
Rådhuspladsen		

Don't miss

Rosenborg Palace

*A picture-postcard pleasure palace
in the heart of the city.*

This little regal residence in the centre of town has just about everything you'd want from a castle. There are sweeping gardens, umpteen royal portraits, exquisite Chinese porcelain, endlessly receding corridors, intriguing nooks, crannies and turrets, and stunningly pompous thrones made from narwhal tusks and silver. The most impressive objects of all are the regal bling of the Danish crown jewels found in the basement, including King Christian IV's crown from the late 16th century – a dense cluster of pearls and stones – as well as jewellery shimmering with diamonds, emeralds and rubies.

There's real charm to the gabled brick exterior, and it's easy to understand why King Christian IV favoured the palace, which he had built in the early 1600s as a summerhouse; it later became a place to receive state visitors. The king's Winter Room, from where the drawbridge was raised and lowered, is richly wood-panelled and decked out with inlaid portraits; a speaking tube in this room allowed the king to place orders to his wine cellar. You can also see the king's lavish writing room, his stuccoed and panelled bedroom and beautifully tiled bathroom.

The surrounding Kongens Have (King's Gardens) are the oldest royal gardens in the country, with topiary-lined paths, sculptures, rose gardens and dense herbaceous borders.

📍	🕐	**DKK**
Øster Voldgade 4A	Tues–Sun 10am–4pm	115
🚇		**W**
Nørreport		kongernessamling.dk/en/ rosenborg

Don't miss

Nationalmuseet (National Museum of Denmark)

Ancient burials, Viking jewels and voices from the past.

The country's keynote museum is housed in an elegant former royal palace, whose interior courtyard is thoroughly swish and modern. With galleries leading in all directions, this is the place to explore Danish history, from the Bronze Age and the Vikings to Denmark today. In its depth and range, the museum also expresses something about the unique and free-thinking soul of the nation.

Perhaps the most fascinating section is on Danish antiquity, where the major exhibits include the 3000-year-old Trundholm sun chariot, a stylised bronze horse pulling a gilded disc. It's thought that the sculpture may have functioned as a mind-blowingly early calendar. Elsewhere, a Bronze Age tree-trunk coffin holds the touching remains of the famous Egtved Girl, whose clothes survived thousands of years of burial remarkably intact.

There are, as you would expect, great hauls of jewellery and weaponry from the Viking era, as well as artefacts from more peaceable times: the street of 19th-century doll's houses is a particularly lovely sight. There's even a hash stand from Christiania (see p.113) in the Stories of Denmark gallery, which shows artefacts from 1660 to 2000 and shines a light on the unique makeup of the country. The Voices from the Colonies exhibit focuses on the people once enslaved in the former Danish colonies: both their suffering and their resistance.

📍	🕐	DKK
Ny Vestergade 10	Tues–Sun 10am–5pm	95
🚌		W
Rådhuspladsen / Gammel Strand		en.natmus.dk

Don't miss

Nyhavn

Picture-perfect Copenhagen: painted buildings,
quay-side boats and a fairytale past.

You may well recognise these two rows of brightly painted 17th-century houses facing each other across a long skinny harbour, as they've become an emblem of the city. The harbour was built between 1670 and 1675 by Swedish prisoners of war under the orders of King Christian V and was once something of a red-light district, with boozed up sailors looking for some fun.

Nyhavn's bars, cafes and pedestrian streets get packed with visitors, to the extent that the Copenhagen Tourist Board has given up promoting this as an attraction. You'd be missing out though if you don't see the harbour. Come early to avoid the crowds – you can have morning coffee wrapped in a cafe blanket if need be – and watch the boats bobbing on the water and the coloured facades of amber, baby blue and citrus light up.

If you're on the Hans Christian Andersen trail, have a peek at number 20 where he lived from 1834–38 and wrote his first fairytales – *The Princess and the Pea, The Tinderbox* and *Little Claus and Big Claus*. The improbable story goes that Hans' landlady would pour water on the neighbouring floor so that she and her children could skate round the room. Fed up with such capers, he moved to the Hotel du Nord on Kongens Nytorv but eventually moved back to Nyhavn, lodging at number 67 from 1848–65, and then at number 18, where he made a home on the first floor from 1871 until near the end of his life in 1875.

Nyhavn	N/A	Free

Kongens Nytorv

Don't miss

Rundetaarn (Round Tower)

*Make a gradual ascent of the ramp for
bird's-eye city views.*

There are towers to climb all over Europe, but this spiralling tower has a
ramp, rather than the usual staircase, built so that a horse and cart could
bring books and equipment into the upper chambers. The story goes that
Peter the Great rode his horse up here. Built in the 17th century by King
Christian IV, this impressive structure initially functioned as an observatory.
It's now just a viewing tower, but it's well worth the (small) fee to take the
gently spiralling walk to get to the top. The handsome construction features
brick floors and whitewashed vaulted ceilings, and ingeniously reaches its
elevation without too much exertion on your part: you walk 209 metres (685
feet) to reach a height of 39 metres (128 feet) and stand on an outdoor deck
for 360 degree views of the whole city centre.

   Towards the top, stop off at the library hall (now empty of books),
which once housed the university's book collection and welcomed Hans
Christian Andersen as a reader. The library hall is now a gallery and a space
for concerts, and has a souvenir and coffee shop. The top of the tower is
given an extra vertiginous edge by the glass floor, through which you can
look down into the hollow core.

		DKK
Købmagergade 52A	Daily 10am–6pm	25
	Tues & Wed 10am–9pm	
	(Apr–Sept)	**W**
Nørreport /	Tues & Wed 10am–9pm	rundetaarn.dk/en
Kongens Nytorv	Thurs–Sun 10am–6pm	
	(Oct–Mar)	

Don't miss

Arbejdermuseet (The Workers Museum)

*The city's working life explored in the
splendid Workers Assembly Hall.*

If you'd like an antidote to royal Copenhagen, the earthy Workers Museum could be just the thing. The building was constructed in 1879 as an assembly hall, and for me the highlight is the unexpectedly dramatic central chamber with its encircling balcony, shining glass ceiling, wide 1929 chandelier, carved wooden reliefs and fluttering red flags. Lenin and Rosa Luxemburg both visited, and the nation's labour unions met here to hammer out the laws that ensured fair conditions for the country's workers.

Upstairs, the transplanted interior of a working class Østerbro home pays sweet homage to the Sorensen family, who moved to the two-room apartment in 1915 with five grown-up children. An original 1950s coffee bar serves Danish chocolate biscuit cake and Rich's Coffee Substitute, which floods older locals with nostalgia. Downstairs, a modern exhibit explores the nature of modern work, though in its content and presentation it has more to offer to local visitors than tourists. Café & Øl-halle "1892" (see p.31) is also in the basement here.

Rømersgade 22	Thurs–Tues 10am–4pm Wed 10am–7pm	**DKK** 75
 Nørreport		**W** arbejdermuseet.dk

Don't miss

Christiania

*Leafy and free: the hippie zone
in the heart of the city.*

Founded by squatters on the site of a former military district when the city was in the midst of an affordable housing crisis in 1971, Christiania is a free-spirited city within the city. Walking down Pusher Street – where soft drugs are openly sold (and illegal) and photography is definitely not welcome – you might feel that the hippie dream has faded. There are some visibly strung-out characters, and the cluster of bars and restaurants can feel more hassly than eco-friendly. But beyond the main (pedestrian) lanes you'll find that a green spirit still lives here, amongst around a thousand permanent members of the intentional community. Ingeniously self-built eco-homes sit in lush gardens sheltered by mature trees and, while it's obviously good practice to respect the residents' privacy, visitors can wander the car-free streets.

    The district was the birthplace of the Christiania cargo bike, a front-loaded carrier of children, pets, partners and furniture, which Princess Mary uses to ferry her children to school. An all-female blacksmiths, Kvindesmedien, sells some handsome pieces, from colourful metal shelves to twirly candelabras, and music venue Nemoland invites the whole city to free weekend gigs in summer. Jazzclub (see p.69) is a lovely low-key venue for jazz-lovers.

Christiania	N/A	**DKK** Free
Christianshavn		**W** christiania.org

Don't miss

The Little Mermaid

Small in stature but a huge cultural icon.

Rather like the *Mona Lisa*, this small and unassuming artwork can feel underwhelming, but nonetheless it has become a symbol of the city. Sitting pretty on her rock, the modest *Little Mermaid* has received some rough treatment over the years from various activist groups. She's been decapitated three times, doused in paint and has even been blown off her perch with explosives. You'll have to be up at the crack of dawn to commune with the mermaid on your own: the wee statue, now backed by the wind turbines and industrial structures of Refshaleøen, is very much on the tourist trail, and the rocks on which she sits are generally thronged. It's easy to walk here or you can get a sea view of the maid on the Hey Captain boat tours (see p.91).

The bronze statue was created by Edvard Eriksen in homage to Hans Christian Andersen's 1837 fable, in which a mermaid falls in love with a human prince. Her decision to surrender her marine existence to be with him has tragic consequences, which may come as a shock to those familiar with the Disney version of the tale.

⚲	⊙	**DKK**
Langelinie	N/A	Free
⊟		**W**
Østerport		heycaptain.dk

Don't miss

NATURE
IN THE CITY

Copenhagen is a city with a strong spiritual connection to nature, evidenced in its enhanced eco-consciousness. While winter hygge is all about the snug indoors, summer hygge is about immersion in nature. Wherever you go you'll see locals swimming, kayaking, cycling, running and steeping themselves in the urban outdoors. Year-round, more than 60 per cent of commutes are by bike, and you can join the locals on the city's dedicated cycle lanes (see p. 123), many enclosed by greenery.

For those looking for an adrenaline-charged swim, bathe in one of the well-designed harbour pools, such as at Islands Brygge (see p. 133). For a relaxing sauna followed by a meal from an onsite kitchen garden, go to La Banchina (see p. 125) – my favourite spot in the city. A very Copenhagen experience can be found at Copenhot (see p. 127), known for its hot tubs with a view, including a 'sailing' hot tub – inventive Danish hygge at its best.

City swimming

*Make like a local and jump into the harbour
waters or head east to the sea.*

Following a decade-long clean-up programme, the wide waters of
Copenhagen harbour make for idyllic swimming. On summer days it can
feel like the whole city is in their swimming gear and on the waterfront,
with exuberant and fearless folk diving in and bathing in the salt waters.
    There are three harbour pools in the city, the most famous being
at Islands Brygge (see p.133). On the opposite bank at Fisketorvet you'll find
an Olympic-sized outdoor pool, plus sections for divers and kids, and there's
a third option at Sluseholmen. Otherwise, officially speaking, you're only
supposed to swim where you see yellow buoys. But this is
free-thinking Copenhagen, where nobody seems too bothered by such rules.
The area with decking by North Atlantic House (see p.145) is a prime spot,
and the slippery scenic jetty at La Banchina (see p.125) is another. Even
where you see the buoys there are no lifeguards, except at Islands
Brygge pool.
    If you fancy a sea swim, head out to the Amager Strandpark, the
largest beach in the city, or try the beautiful sea bath at Kastrup, a circular
timber structure that's ideal for diving and summery lounging and has won
awards for its bold design.

📍	🕐	**DKK**
Various locations	Hours vary	Free

Nature in the city

Butterfly House

Beautiful butterflies dart amongst exotic blooms.

Gothersgade 128

Nørreport

Tues–Sun 10am–5pm
(April–Oct)

DKK
60

W
botanik.snm.ku.dk

On a rainy day in Copenhagen, it's worth seeking out some tropical hygge in the enchanting Butterfly House in the Botanic Gardens. The air in the hot house dances with butterflies, which frequently land on visitors: most common are the black and red Postman species, but dark orange Julia butterflies flit by, and the blue batik wings of the Airnome cracker are another delight. Occasionally huge Peleides blue morphos beat the air with their irridescent wings, then settle on a leaf and close up in favour of mottled brown obscurity. Orchids, aloes and rare desert plants make for the loveliest of settings, and it's fascinating to watch the butterflies emerge from their pupae.

The ticket also includes entry to the sensual year-round Palm House, a 19th-century glasshouse filled with tropical flowers and giant bamboo.

Geological Museum

Get up close to the earth's treasures.

Øster Voldgade 5–7

35 32 22 22

Nørreport

Tues–Sun 10am–5pm

DKK

105

W

geologi.snm.ku.dk/english

This red brick monolith houses a somewhat old-fashioned museum, with a cabinet-of-curiosities approach to curation. But it also hosts some very cool exhibitions, which bring things right up to date. My recent favourite was a temporary meteorite exhibit, where you could touch a moon rock and a chunk of meteor and play star-catching via several interactive displays.

The permanent collections mainly comprise wonderfully varied rocks and crystals, sitting in long rows in glassed cases, as well as fluorescent minerals, Icelandic zeolite and calcite, Kongsberg silver and Baltic amber. The museum's display of pinned butterflies makes a rather sad contrast with the fluttering living beauties at the nearby Butterfly House (see p.120), but they're here for a reason: the curators are keen to stress the message that these fragile creatures send us about climate change when their numbers fall. There's also a brand-new permanent dinosaur exhibit on the way.

Nature in the city

Cycling

*Commute with bike-loving Copenhageners
on dedicated cycle paths.*

Copenhagen is famous for its devotion to sporty two-wheeled transport. Everybody cycles here, from parents pedalling clusters of kids crammed into cargo bikes to senior citizens. Bikes can be hired at many spots, including Christiania Rent A Bike, where options include the high-framed Pedersen Bicycle, and at Copenhagen Bicycles on Nyhavn.

Bike rental companies hire out sturdy upright bikes, which have front brakes on the handlebar and a back brake which engages when you pedal backwards, something which takes a bit of practice if you're not use to it. You can also hire an electric bike from Bycyklen.

Throughout the city, you'll find separate cycle lanes with their own dedicated traffic lights, but the cycle lanes during rush hours can be a little intense for rookie cyclists. If you're feeling nervous, keep to the right and allow the locals to whizz by. And look out for bus stops, where passengers disembark into the cycle paths: if in doubt, stop to let people cross to the pavement. There are also the wonderful Green Cycle Routes, which cut leafy corridors for 60 kilometres (37 miles) through and around the city via parks, disused rail lines, lake shores and playing fields. Pick up the Cycling Map Copenhagen at the Visit Copenhagen office (Vesterbrogade 4).

Christiana Rent a Bike	Copenhagen Bicycles
Mon–Fri 9am–5.30pm	Mon–Sat 9.30am–6pm
Sat 11am–3pm	(Hours vary in summer)
W	**W**
christianacykler.dk/rent-a-bike	copenhagenbicycles.dk

Nature in the city

La Banchina

*A low-key sauna, kitchen garden and cafe
with the mantra of dip, eat, repeat.*

Welcome to my favourite place in the city, where outdoorsy Danish style is
at its best. La Banchina is a blue-painted shack with its own jetty, which is a
jumping off point for idyllic summer swims in the harbour. Last time I visited,
intending a coffee and a quick dip, I lost a couple of hours to languid chats in
their wooden barrel sauna, whose perfect circle shape is glassed at one end
so that you can lie watching boats nip past and the surrounding branches
shake in the breeze.

In the small garden they grow produce for a commendable little onsite
kitchen, which dishes up pastries, French toast with Danish blueberries and
baked fish dishes, all served on blue-rimmed white metal plates. They serve
breakfast, then a simple lunch/early dinner menu; you can sit inside the
shack or under the trees on benches in warmer weather. Service is a little
slow but speed isn't the point here.

You don't need a sauna reservation – just show up. When it's cold
outside, throw another log on the fire, splash the coals with water from the
wooden pail and feel your limbs melt. Even in the colder months, it's fun to
alternate lying in the heat with plunges into the harbour water from the jetty.
If you've ever wondered why Danes have such healthy glowing skin ... this
could be the answer.

⚲	⊙	**DKK**
Refshalevej 141	Mon–Sun 8am–8pm	Sauna 50
		Food 65–115
🚌		
2A		**W**
		labanchina.dk

Nature in the city

Copenhot

Dunk yourself in a hot tub or view the harbour from a floating wellness spa.

Copenhot is a typically Copenhagen creative and fun project: a collection of hot tubs and sauna sheds sitting on the water at the far northern edge of super-cool Refshaleøen, which aims to bring a wilderness vibe to the city. Their concept is new Nordic wellness, and the hot tubs and saunas use clean seawater and firewood for heat.

The most affordable option is a 'hot day' package, where guests share the hot tubs or a panoramic sauna with a gorgeous view of *The Little Mermaid* (see p.115); the idea is to mix folk together and to promote sociability amongst guests. Otherwise, you can rent the rocket-like tower hot tub at the centre of the complex, enjoy your own rustic sauna hut, or hire a circular tub for yourself and friends.

The wackiest option – and the most expensive – is the sailing hot tub, which allows you to bob around the harbour steered by a Copenhot sailor, whilst wallowing in 40°C (104°F) clean saltwater. All these activities can, of course, be alternated with harbour plunges in true healthy Danish style. Book at least 24 hours ahead for all these activities.

Refshalevej 325
31 32 78 08

2A, harbour bus

Wed–Sun 10am–10pm

DKK
300–2200

W
copenhot.com

Nature in the city

Blocs & Walls

Join sport-mad Danes and climb indoors or outdoors.

Refshalevej 163D

32 57 25 00

9A

Mon–Fri 10am–11pm
Sat 10am–8pm
Sun 10am–10pm

DKK
Daypass 130

W
blocs-walls.dk/en

This funky climbing centre in the transforming industrial district of Refshaleøen is best reached via a leisurely cycle ride from the city centre. Once inside, you can ascend 15-metre-high walls and get expert instruction on rope climbing and bouldering; if you haven't got the right kind of shoes with you, just rent them from the centre for DKK 40.

Personally, I prefer having a more modest clamber on the centre's outdoor wall, edged by trees and grasses, where it's easier to pretend you're shimmying up a real rockface. There's a cafe inside, but if you're hungry after your exertions it's best to head to acclaimed street food market Reffen (see p.52), a short stroll away.

Frederiksberg Gardens & Palace

Herons, elephants and summer boat trips.

Several Entrances
Frederiksberg Palace tours

36 13 26 32

Frederiksberg Allé

Mon–Sun 6am–9pm

DKK
Free

These vast gardens were the favourite pleasure park of early 18th-century monarch Frederik VI, whose statue sits at the main entrance. Peachy yellow Frederiksberg Palace (guided tours last Sat of each month), his summer retreat, is perched on a summit overlooking the canals and avenues of the park, which are colonised by grey herons. The little 1803 Chinese pavilion was Frederik's tea house and he was ferried round the waterways in a gondola. Today a boat company runs summer trips on the park's lake, in homage to the monarch.

The city's historic zoo is also here. One of the oldest zoos in Europe, it houses Nordic animals, such as grey wolves, reindeer and brown bears, as well as Asian elephants, hippos and a Tasmanian area – complete with Tasmanian Devils – which was inaugurated when the Prince of Denmark married Tasmanian Mary Donaldson in 2004.

Nature in the city

Dronning Louises Bro (Queen Louise's Bridge) & The Lakes

A lovely low-key green area to catch a flavour of the city at play.

Between Nørrebrogaden (Nørrebro) and Frederiksborggade (city centre)

Norreport /
Trianglen /
Forum

DKK
Free

Queen Louise's Bridge, lined with wrought-iron lanterns, is an essential city meeting spot, spanning the lake between Nørrebro and the city centre. The bridge, whose wide cycle lanes are crossed by a steady stream of cyclists, is punctuated by benches, where Copenhageners hang out in summer. You can join the locals and jog, cycle and, on weekends, rent a swan-shaped pedalo from the booth near the north end of the bridge.

The three long lakes here once formed a natural stream. Having served as reservoirs in the 18th century, they are now integral to local leisure. The water here isn't as clean as that in the harbour (see p.91) so swimming isn't advised (or legal).

Assistens Cemetery

This cemetery is a surprisingly social spot.

Several Entrances

Nørrebros Runddel

Mon–Sun 7am–10pm

DKK
Free

W
assistens.dk

In Copenhagen it seems that the refreshingly straightforward approach to life also applies to death. Assistens Cemetery is very much a used, loved park, where locals picnic in summer, and stroll and cycle the avenues year-round. The cemetery was opened in 1760, originally as a pauper graveyard, but its long avenues and spacious lawns made it a fashionable burial spot from the Golden Age onwards.

There are a few 'celebrity' graves: those of Hans Christian Andersen (in the bottom south corner), Danish philosopher Søren Kierkegaard (also at the south end, but closer to Nørrebrogade), Afro-American jazz musicians Ben Webster and Kenny Drew who lived in the city, and Danish physicist Niels Bohr who was instrumental in developing quantum theory. At the south-western edge, the old stable buildings house the Herman Stilling Museum (Sat & Sun 1–5pm June–Sept), honouring a painter known for his bright naïve paintings of trolls.

Nature in the city

Islands Brygge pool

Jump right into the city's most hyggelige harbour pool.

It's a tribute to Copenhagen's clean water that this handsome timber pool sits pretty much in the centre of it, just over the water from the city's main sights. It's brilliantly designed, with five separate pools, two of them for children, as well as three diving boards (one metre, three metres and a giddy five metres). Lifeguards occupy the jaunty red-and-white striped booth that recalls the funnel of an ocean liner. Water quality is regularly checked, and if there's any doubt about it a red flag is raised to advise swimmers.

In summer this is a cheerful riot of paddling kids, diving teens and locals doing laps alongside visitors – bathing whilst the yellow harbour bus boats (see p.91) and pleasure boats nip by is unforgettable. In winter, the pool is reserved for a local swimming club: a hardy group of Copenhageners who plough up and down, whatever the weather.

Islands Brygge 14
30 89 04 69

Islands Brygge

Daily 10am–6pm
(Mid-May–mid-Sept)

DKK
Free

W
svoemkbh.kk.dk/
havnebade

Nature in the city

DESIGNER DANES

Danes have been design conscious for longer than most, and around the city you'll see wonderful attention to design detail. Danish architecture is famous the world over, from the all-encompassing vision of Arne Jacobsen and the striking Royal Danish Library (Black Diamond, see p.139) and Operaen (The Royal Opera, see p.147) to wildly experimental buildings springing up in the new district of Nordhavn and across the open spaces of Amager.

The approach of designers and architects, perhaps driven by the nation's social conscience and egalitarianism, is very much on people-centred projects rather than remote minimalism. Leisure activities, fitness and communality are embedded in the design process, an extraordinary example being the new eco power station and ski slope, CopenHill (see p.149), and umpteen innovations that make life easier and safer for the city's cyclists, such as the Bicycle Snake (see p.153). Indeed, this forward-thinking nation is leading the conversation about eco building – you can find out much more about this at the Design Museum Danmark (see p.137) and BLOX (see p.143).

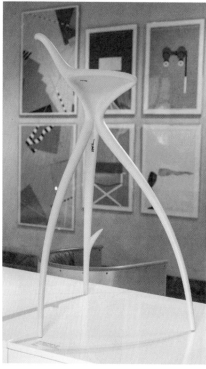

Design Museum Danmark

Explore the spiritual home of Danish design.

Created way back in 1890 and housed in a stately former hospital, the city's Design Museum is anything but old-fashioned. The light-filled halls illuminate Danish innovation, in particular the country's increasing focus on sustainability. You'll find challenging displays on cities of the future and an examination of how architecture and design can be resilient and flexible in the face of climate change.

Most of the displays are on the spacious ground floor, in connected rooms that enclose a central tree-lined courtyard. The first galleries you encounter are devoted to domestic items and gadgets, varying in style from muted mid-century modernism to colourful 1980s kitsch. Beyond is the eco-focussed section, with items including a bamboo bike and a futuristic outfit created from recycled straws. Bright posters and prints bedeck the furniture gallery, and there's a special hall that displays top-lit Danish chairs. Beyond, you'll find items from the museum's early collections, including Lalique vases and elegant 18th-century Japanese crafts, while upstairs there's a display of porcelain, which includes the earliest productions of Royal Copenhagen (see p.163).

It's well worth factoring in time for lunch at the museum's cafe Klint (see p.32), which has tables outside and an attractive salon. The museum store sells a desirable selection of gifts, including Danish ceramics and clothing, postcards, publications and posters.

⚲	⊙	**DKK**
Bredgade 68	Tues–Sun 10am–5pm	115
🚌		**W**
Marmorkirken		designmuseum.dk/en

Designer Danes

Royal Danish Library (Black Diamond)

Catch a photography show at this dramatic harbour building.

When it was decided that the royal library needed a new building, the city of Copenhagen didn't go for a traditional stuffy design but, typically, for a boldly modern and striking one. Completed in 1999 and designed by Schmidt Hammer Lassen Architects, the Black Diamond, as the library is known, sits right on the waterfront on Slotsholmen. The dramatically angled building is faced with black polished granite, reflecting the sea and sky and gleaming on even the dullest day, while the interior consists of sinuous tiered galleries lit by a huge glassed atrium.

The library houses a collection of nearly all the books published in the country since 1482, but is particularly known for holding the archive of philosopher Søren Kierkegaard and the correspondence of Hans Christian Andersen. Books need to be ordered in advance and are accessible in special reading rooms. But while the shelves are off-limits for people studying, many visitors come to admire the architecture of the central hall, which is open to everyone, and to check out one of the changing exhibitions of the National Museum of Photography. There's also a bookshop, a cafe and the impressive Dronningesalen concert hall that seats 600 and hosts classical concerts, talks and movie screenings.

Weekly tours (Mondays at 3pm) take visitors round the original 1906 library building, as well as the glittering diamond itself.

◉	⌄	DKK
Søren Kierkegaards Plads 1	Mon–Fri 8am–8pm	Free entry
	Sat 9am–6pm	Tours 60
	Tours Mon 3pm	
🚆		W
Christianshavn / Gammel Strand		kb.dk

Designer Danes

Kunsthal Charlottenborg

Discover new Danish artists and admire global art stars.

Nyhavn 2

Kongens Nytorv

Tues–Fri 12pm–8pm
Sat & Sun 11am–5pm

DKK
90

W
kunsthalcharlottenborg.dk/en

It's well worth heading away from crowded Nyhavn (see p.107) to this peaceful courtyard gallery. The late 17th-century palace buildings here are some of the loveliest in the city, forming a handsome square wreathed in ivy, which takes on a burnished red-orange colour in autumn.

Since 1883, Kunsthal Charlottenborg has focussed on nurturing new talent, Danish and international, and providing a space for established art stars. Its super-inclusive spring show is open to all fine artists, while from April–May you can check out the graduate degree show of the Royal Danish Academy of Fine Arts. At other times there's an impressive roster of changing exhibitions, and the gallery also runs a strong programme of fun culture nights, talks, film screenings and performances: check out its website for details. The onsite Motto Bookstore has an excellent selection of art books and magazines. Combine your art viewing with lunch or a drink at neighbouring Apollo Bar (see p.35).

Nyboder

This secluded fairytale streetscape endures in the heart of the city.

Sankt Pauls Gade 24

Østerport / Marmorkirken

N/A

DKK

Free

I first stumbled on this network of streets by accident and couldn't believe that such fairytale beauty survived intact in the city centre. Nyboder is composed of terraces of ochre-meets-tangerine-coloured cottages, which march in identical rows down the cobbled streets, with neat sage-green doors and sash windows and plum-coloured wooden shutters. Their steep terracotta-tiled roofs are topped with chimneys and every home has a cluster of bikes parked outside.

This lovely vision was conceived by King Christian IV; the cottages were built for sailors who lived in them between 1631 and 1795. They are currently undergoing a major street-by-street restoration and are still occupied by navy, army and air force personnel, though civilians can also apply to live here. Go and see for yourself: you'll feel like you're stepping into the pages of a Hans Christian Andersen story.

Designer Danes

BLOX

Architects local and global take
centre stage at BLOX.

The 2018 BLOX building occupies the site of the former royal brewhouse and was conceived by Dutch starchitect Rem Koolhaas as a city within a city, for learning, eating, discussion and play. It houses the Danish Architecture Centre (DAC), Copenhagen's showcase of architecture, design and new ideas, as well as apartments and a gym. BLOX sits on the harbour near the Black Diamond Library (see p.139) and is well worth a visit if you're interested in the inspired city planning that Copenhagen has become famous for.

On the ground floor of the centre there's a homage to the building blocks of future architects: Lego. Many of the city's key buildings, such as CopenHill (see p.149), have been recreated in Lego here and there's a huge collection for kids to play with. On the second floor, a combination of architectural models, plans, photos and films form a dramatic and colourful exploration of building in the city and beyond. Explore the creation of local projects such as Cykelslangen (see p.153), the harbour baths (see p.119) and the 8Tallet apartment complex on Amager, and discover how major world cities are utilising Danish architects and design concepts. A short film explores the very special human-centred nature of the country's design.

On the top floor you can enjoy coffee, cake and harbour views in the BLOX cafe. And, on weekends from May to September, DAC operate lunchtime architectural walking tours of some of Copenhagen's modern buildings.

Bryghuspladsen

Christianshavn /
Gammel Strand

Mon–Wed & Fri–Sun
10am–6pm
Thurs 10am–9pm

DKK

DAC entry 115
Tours 125

W

blox.dk/English
dac.dk/en

Designer Danes

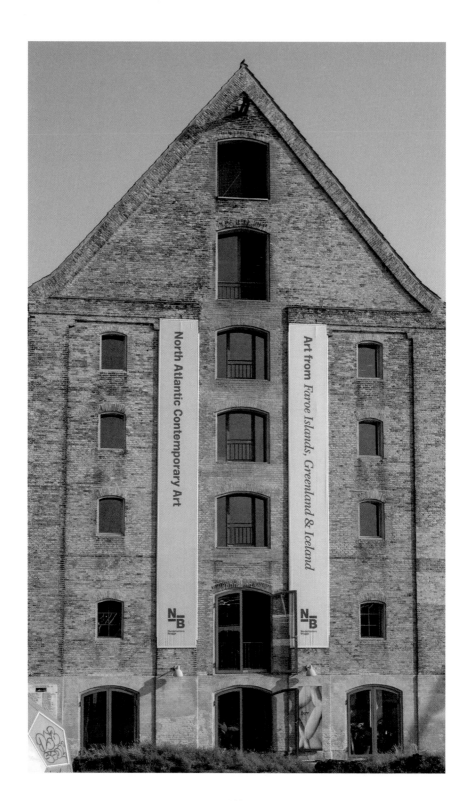

North Atlantic House

Discover the city's trading and artistic links
with its northern neighbours.

I have to declare a personal interest in this bluff 1767 warehouse, with its exposed beams and plank floors: I once lived for a month in another lovely old building close by and regularly swam in the warehouse harbour, where ships from chilly north Atlantic ports once docked. The huge building houses various North Atlantic-related organisations, including the Icelandic Embassy, as well as acclaimed Nordic cuisine restaurant Barr (see p.45), but you can also explore the excellent contemporary art gallery on the ground floor, as well as thoughtful displays on each landing.

The gallery reflects the fine art and culture of Greenland, Iceland and the Faroe Islands – former Danish colonies-turned-trading partners. Exhibits delve into issues such as how climate change is affecting the Inuit people, or how the region's folk art intersects with the contemporaryart world. The landing displays include a ginormous copper pot once used to boil whale blubber and descriptions of the items stored here during the bygone trading era: dried and salted fish, whale oil, seal skins, polar bear and Artic fox fur, dried fish, bird feathers, eiderdown, reindeer horn, narwhal teeth, refined sulphur and wool.

Strandgade 91

Kongens Nytorv

$\bigodot$

Mon–Fri 10am–5pm
Sat & Sun 12pm–5pm

DKK

Free

W

nordatlantens.dk/en

Designer Danes

Operaen (The Royal Opera)

*Have a night at the opera or take a tour
of the bold waterfront building.*

Possibly the second most dramatically sited opera house in the world
(after Sydney), this eccentric edifice sits on the waterfront on Holmen,
surrounded by yachts and ferries and backed by cruise ships. Topped by a
flat roof, which juts out confidently towards the water, Operaen is home to
the limestone-clad Royal Danish Opera. Walking in you'll be knocked out by
the light-flooded interior with its Sicilian marble floor, while the concert hall
itself is cocooned in an internal shell of maple wood. The ceiling of the main
auditorium glitters with 105,000 sheets of 24-carat gold.

The building was funded by shipping magnate Arnold Mærsk Mc-Kinney
Møller, who dictated many aspects of the building's appearance, though
Henning Larsen is credited as the architect. Their testy relationship and other
nuggets are revealed on fascinating opera house tours (75 minutes).

In a weird footnote, despite being almost totally flat, this sporty city
has managed to take part in international cliff diving championships by having
participants jump from the roof of the opera house into the harbour waters.

 DKK

Ekvipagemestervej 10   Hours vary   Tours 135
Tickets 123–435

2A Harbour bus   **W**
kglteater.dk/en

Designer Danes

CopenHill

*Only in Copenhagen: green power meets
adventure sports.*

You simply cannot miss this huge new building on Refshaleøen, which opened
in 2019: a tall triangle punctuated with slim towers which periodically puff
out steam. This is a power station but one with a very Danish difference.
It's a waste-to-energy plant, thought to be the cleanest power station in
the world, and forms a significant part of the city's plans to become carbon
neutral by 2025. In this, as in so much else, Copenhagen is leading the way.

But not content with being future-focussed, clean and green, the
designers of CopenHill, Bjarke Ingels Group (BIG), decided to throw in
some fun and make the project about human energy as well as eco-energy.
Pancake-flat Denmark now rivals its Nordic neighbours by having its own
ski slopes and recreational hiking area, built into the angled side of CopenHill.

Here you can ski and snowboard, plus there's space for running
and hiking up the grassed slopes. And the exterior of the structure also
incorporates the world's highest climbing wall, a giddy 85 metres (280 feet)
tall and 10 metres (33 feet) wide. After your exertions, an après ski bar awaits
at the bottom of the slopes where you can enjoy drinks and snacks.

📍	🕐	**DKK**
Vindmøllevej 6	Mon–Tues & Thurs–Fri	Hourly ski pass from 50
	12pm–8pm	Equipment hire 150
	Wed 12pm–10pm	
2A	Sat 10am–8pm	**W**
	Sun 10am–6pm	copenhill.dk/en

Contemporary Copenhagen

Modern art installations in a hipster hangar.

A huge Refshaleøen hangar, once a shipyard welding hall, plays host to this modern gallery, now fronted by a neon sign reading CC. The focus is on installation work, with the vast gallery space providing an airy and flexible canvas for artists – which have in the past included Yoko Ono, Bruce Nauman and Anselm Kiefer – to play with.

Refshalevej 173A

Contemporary Copenhagen specialises in getting visitors actively involved in the exhibitions, through guided tours, art walks, talks, concerts and workshops. Check the website to see the program and book ahead for tours.

2A

Wed & Fri–Sun 11am–6pm
Thurs 11am–9pm

The super-cool shop sells art books, jewellery, ceramics and skin-care products. For a bite to eat and a craft ale after your art viewing, pop next door to Broaden & Build (see p.73).

DKK

100

W

copenhagencontemporary.
org/en

Cisterns

Subterranean art experience across from Frederiksberg Palace.

Bag Søndermarken

Enghave Place / Frederiksberg Allé

Tues–Sun 11am–6pm

DKK
Varies

W
cisternerne.dk/en

This is an eccentric attraction and an oddly enjoyable one. The 19th-century cisterns under the lawns of Søndermarken were once a reservoir, containing 16 million litres of drinking water. In 2019 they were transformed into an atmospheric exhibit by art collective SUPERFLEX, which envisaged a future drowned world. Each year a different artist or group will install a new experience here; check online to see if you have to book in advance.

Two glassed pyramids serve as portals to the cisterns – you descend into them via steps and then change your shoes for wellingtons (gumboots): the water throughout the cisterns is several inches deep. You're then free to wander the very dimly lit chambers, where faint coloured lights shimmer in the water and the ambient sound of dripping and the sloshing of fellow visitors creates a unique and somewhat sinister ambience.

Den Frie (Centre of Contemporary Art)

*Pioneering performance
and contemporary art.*

Oslo Pl

Østerport

Tues–Wed & Fri–Sun
12pm–6pm
Thurs 12pm–9pm

DKK
70

W
denfrie.dk/en

Located away from the centre in leafy Østerbro, the Den Frie is dedicated to the arts and architecture. It was founded by a group of artists way back in 1898, in opposition to what they saw as the stuffy annual art show at Kunsthal Charlottenborg (see p.140). The lovely wooden building, designed by one of Den Frie's founders, pioneering Danish Art Nouveau architect J.F. Willumsen, has a temple-like entrance and a gilded Pegasus frieze over the door, inspired by ancient Greek culture. The structure, which was moved to this location in 1913, is as much of an attraction as the changing exhibits.

With the strong commitment to experimental art of its founders still intact, Den Frie seeks to connect artists and audiences. The Polykrom cafe is a low-key but pleasant spot to restore with coffee and cake.

The Circle Bridge & Bicycle Snake

Cycle or walk across this artist-designed bridge.

Johan Semps Gade

Christianshavn

DKK
Free

When the city decided to build a new pedestrian bridge to connect Christiansbro and Appelbys Plads and open up the inner harbour, it was never going to be a boring old arch. Instead they called on Icelandic artist Olafur Eliasson to deliver something a bit different. Eliasson designed five circular connecting platforms, each one topped by a tall mast that recalls the shipfaring history of the city. Cirkelbroen (The Circle Bridge) opened in 2015 and has become a much loved Copenhagen landmark.

If this gives you a taste for the city's bridges, try cycling across Cykelslangen (Bicycle Snake), south of the centre. This elevated cycleway, surfaced in vibrant orange, takes you on a sinuous route from Dybbølsbro bridge, over Fisketorvet harbour bath and down to Bryggebroen, another cycle bridge which leads across the harbour.

MUST-BUYS
+ MARKETS

With a preoccupation for thoughtful design, Copenhagen is a paradise for discerning shoppers and you'll discover individual pieces, such as jewellery at House of Amber (see p. 161) and Georg Jensen (see p. 168), stylish homewares, cool clothing and elegant ceramics. The city has plenty of quirky individual stores to keep you and your home dressed in a Danish aesthetic. The centre of the city features the historic Royal Copenhagen store (see p. 163) and other gems, while Nørrebro is the place for funkier shopping, specifically super-hip Jægersborggade (see p. 173). Museum and gallery shops are generally outstanding, too.

In the warmer months markets, such as Kongens Nytorv (see p. 170) and Veras Market (see p. 171) sell antiques and vintage gear, while in winter Christmas market magic grips the city in seasonal hygge heaven. TorvehallerneKBH market (see p. 157) is a must-visit for seasonal produce any time of the year.

TorvehallerneKBH market

*Stroll the stalls for seasonal fruits and sugarcane
superjuice at this covered market.*

To immerse yourself in Copenhagen's foodie culture, head to TorvehallerneKBH, the glassed-over market, where you can start your day at Grød, which means porridge. They serve healthy Danish breakfasts: try the three-grain porridge, chia seed pudding with plum compote, or the açai blueberry bowl with Grød granola. If you need caffeine, the Coffee Collective is a great stop; for a sweet treat Laura's Bakery serves up sourdough and classic Danish potato cakes; and Granny's House home-bakes everything from apple cakes with sour cream to jams for their tarts.

You'll find specialty vendors selling oils, spices, chocolates and other goodies. I generally make a beeline for the ethical Ugandic stall, where the Ugandan owner crushes sugarcane and combines it with lime and passionfruit juice served in biodegradable cups. Their no-added-sugar chocolate bars are a sweet treat and the piles of tiny ladyfinger bananas and mangoes bring a sunny vibe to the coldest Copenhagen day.

You can wander for hours here and if you're self-catering this is the spot to stock up on nuts, juices, meats, fish, wine and much more. I love to buy seasonal fruit and vegetables, from spring greens to fat blackberries, blood-red lingonberries and amber-coloured cloudberries in late summer and autumn.

♀	⊘	**W**
Frederiksborggade 21	Mon–Thurs 10am–7pm	torvehallernekbh.dk
	Fri 10am–8pm	
	Sat & Sun 10am–6pm	
Nørreport		

Must-buys + markets

Gun Gun

Artisan gifts handmade in an 18th-century townhouse.

This is my favourite gift shop in Copenhagen, for its fairytale backstory and personal approach. The handsome 18th-century townhouse was owned by an elderly lady, who specified that it should be used for creativity. And in stepped a collective of seven female artists looking for a space to work, collaborate and showcase their diverse creations.

The shop is always staffed by one of the artists – they take it in turns – who can tell you all about their work: Ida Rørholm Davidsen, for example, is an ink and watercolour illustrator who draws magical Copenhagen scenes and images of the natural world; HUNKØN take fashion inspiration from ancient Japan and minimalist Scandinavia; and Häli-Ann Tooms creates dainty devices for plant displays. The shop's pottery is created in-house in the studio behind the till.

Browsing the elegantly arrayed white wooden shelves, you'll see that the only products in the store not made by the collective are fabulous Monkey glasses made in Denmark from biodegradable materials, such as cotton and wood pulp, and handsome handmade bags, also created locally from discarded materials.

Kompagnistæde 25

Gammel Strand

Mon–Fri 11am–6pm
Sat 10am–4pm

W

gungun.dk

Must-buys + markets

House of Amber & Copenhagen Amber Museum

*Treat yourself to some jewels and
marvel at the museum.*

Sited at the point where Nyhavn (see p. 107) meets grand Kongens Nytorv square, this museum and shop occupies one of the oldest buildings in the city: a white-painted 1606 house that predates Nyhavn. Throughout the last 400 years it has been a barber's, a carpenter's, a grocer's shop and a tailor's workshop. It now houses an amber jewellery store on the ground floor and, on the upper floors, a small museum that delves into the story of fossilised tree resin.

The shop itself dates back to 1933 and has a rich selection of jewellery, which gleams in brightly lit glass cabinets. As well as trademark burnished orange, amber comes in green, cherry, cognac and milk hues, which some jewellers combine with bright enamels, as well as with precious stones. There are more than thirty individual lines here, some created in collaboration with designers, such as Maysoun and Lara Bohinc. Styles range from avant-garde to classic to earthy hippy and, as far as prices go, the sky is pretty much the limit. Simpler pieces, such as droplet earrings, start at around €100. The Hidden Treasure collection consists of rare amber with insect and plant inclusions.

Perhaps the most remarkable object in the upstairs museum is the largest piece of amber in the world: a rugged blue-brown hunk that was found by Sumatran miners in 2014. You'll also see 30-million-year-old insects trapped in sap, while amber chess pieces and a model Viking ship with a billowing amber sail show the dexterity with which the 'gold of the north' has been fashioned.

Kongens Nytorv 2,
by Nyhavn

Mon–Sun 10am–6pm
Museum hours vary

W
houseofamber.com

Kongens Nytorv

Must-buys + markets

Royal Copenhagen

Porcelain power at this grand and historic store.

This is one of Denmark's proudest brands, whose white and cobalt-blue painted porcelain has become synonymous with the city. The Royal Copenhagen company was founded in 1775 by Queen Juliane Marie, who also devised the three waves (symbolising three Danish waterways) that are its factory mark. The Blue Fluted Plain range is the iconic one, its botanical design dancing across pure white surfaces, but the company continues to reinvent: Blue Fluted Mega blows up the classic pattern and renders it somewhat abstract, the Flora and Blomst lines are more painterly, while the modern blue and bronze HAV design has a minimal Japanese feel, mimicking fish scales.

Since 1911 the company's flagship store has been in a wonderful three-storey house dating back to 1616. This is much more than a shop though: it provides a history of the company and also, on the top floor which is devoted to the HAV range, takes on more of the feel of an art gallery. On the second floor you might see craftspeople hand-painting pieces with incredibly swift and deft strokes, though they are quite sanguine about the fact that only the top range is painted in-house and that most of the work is now done in Thailand.

Products range from full dinner services to Japanese-inspired teapots, cups and mugs, bowls, jugs and vases.

Amagertorv 6 · Mon–Fri 10am–7pm · royalcopenhagen.com

33 13 71 81 · Sat 10am–6pm

Sun 10am–5pm

Gammel Strand

Must-buys + markets

Pilestræde

Stylish shopping in the centre of the city.

This street cuts a curving swathe through Indre By, or inner city, the affluent heart of Copenhagen, where the best stores sit comfortably in their grand old mansion buildings. While nearby Købmagergade is busier, Pilestræde has got the edge in terms of style.

My personal favourite shops here are Naked (no.46), which stacks women's sneakers in gorgeous contrasting colours, and long-established Heartmade (no.6), which sells flowing and slightly bohemian women's fashion. Oh Dawn (no.47) stocks well-crafted but casual men's clothes and surfboards, while Norse Store (no.41) creates functional yet avant-garde outdoor gear. Handsome lifestyle store NORR (no.36) sits on a corner and displays clothes for men and women, plus shoes, accessories and beauty products. It showcases Danish brands, including Sissel Edelbo, who works vintage Indian fabrics into simple Scandi shapes, and the luxurious feminine fashions of Birgitte Herskind.

The street is ahead of the curve too when it comes to stopping for a bite to eat: 42Raw (no.32) serves colourful raw vegetable dishes, including lush acai bowls and green juices for breakfast, while adjoining Palæo Pilestræde (also no.32) was the world's first entirely paleo restaurant, serving fresh and unprocessed foods.

Pilestræde

Hours vary

Nørreport

Must-buys + markets

Kunst & Håndværk

An earthy craft and gift store with a high hygge rating.

Landemærket 9

Nørreport

Mon–Thurs 11am–5.30pm
Fri 11am–6pm
Sat 11am–4pm

W

kunstoghaandvaerk.com

Kunst & Håndværk means arts and crafts and this lovely store in the city centre near the Round Tower (see p.109) has been selling beautifully crafted objects since 1977. It is run by a cooperative of women artists who display products made by Danish designers and artisans. The ground floor is devoted to homewares and accessories and the first floor to clothing made from soft linen, wool and felt with a wide colour palette.

My favourite things here are the cowl scarves with Baltic amber beads sewn into them by BIRK, the thick wool hats and the unique asymmetrical fitted felt jackets. You'll find ceramics, both rustic and modern, plus a range of jewellery by locally based makers, including Angeles Blanco who creates unique handmade rings and necklaces, and Pia Andersen Smykker who uses vintage materials to create dazzling one-off earrings. There are regular informal events where you can meet the designers who provide the shop with crafts, with drinks and refreshments thrown in.

Rains

*Stay stylishly dry in this
rainy city.*

Unfortunately, rain is likely to be a feature of your visit to Copenhagen. And, whether it's gentle drizzle or a full-on deluge, you'll need something to protect you. This Danish store does a range of waterproof clothing for men and women in a fantastic array of colours, from eye-popping neon and optimistic sunshine yellow to forest green and cobalt blue.

Klareboderne 4

Gammel Strand /
Nørreport

Mon–Fri 10am–6pm
Sat 10am–5pm

W
rains.com

The shapes are very diverse, including cinched-at-the-waist hoodies, capes, puffer jackets and belted macs. This variety, and the unobtrusive branding, means you may not notice that pretty much everyone in the city wears Rains! My partner and I have walked the wet Copenhagen streets together in our Rains jackets, managing not to look like the matching anorak couple. They do bags and other accessories too, including a funky puffer hood with an attached scarf.

Georg Jensen

Modern Danish tableware and jewellery with a distinguished past.

Amagertorv 4

Gammel Strand /
Konggens Nytorv /
Nørreport

Mon–Thurs 10am–6pm
Fri 10am–7pm
Sat & Sun 10am–5pm

W

georgjensen.com/Europe

This is one of the country's most venerable and respected brands: Jensen was a gifted, innovative artisan craftsman, born just north of Copenhagen in 1886, who opened a silversmith's shop on Bredgade in 1904. The launch coincided with the birth of the Art Nouveau movement, and Jensen's flourishing empire was born.

Perhaps the most distinctive pieces today are the stainless-steel candleholders, with their fluid lines and the elegant curving lamp stands. The store also sells classic cutlery and a range of jewellery in rose gold and sterling silver, whose sinuous shapes echo those of the tableware. The company has brought its products bang up to date with The Bed, a sculpted hunk of silverware designed to hold a mobile phone and to symbolically put it to bed and out of reach.

The plain but handsome store sits adjacent to the Royal Copenhagen flagship store (*see* p.163).

Stilleben

Get to grips with Danish style at this interiors store.

Frederiksborggade 22

33 91 11 31

Nørreport

Mon–Fri 10am–6pm

Sat 10am–4pm

W

stilleben.dk

If Danish chic has inspired you and you fancy bringing it into your own home, Stilleben is a great place to start. The brand has had a focus on Danish interior design for more than ten years: the Stilleben store is carefully curated by two female Danish ceramicists, who are expert at selecting the best of local and international design. You'll find furniture, ceramics, original artworks, jewellery and handwoven textiles on the tasteful white and stripped-wood shelves here.

Amongst the Danish design pieces are brightly glazed pots by Studio Arhøj, minimal basketware from Lillerød and the softest of knitware by Kokoon. As well as Tuscan vases, handsome recycled glasses by EcoGlass and American pop art prints.

Stilleben also produces its own accessories, which are an easy take-home, from minimal greetings cards and pretty hairclips to floral shopping totes and candy-striped socks.

Kongens Nytorv market

*Vintage porcelain
and Christmas stalls.*

Kongens Nytorv

Kongens Nytorv

Sat 10am–4pm (May–Sept)

When I'm looking for a special birthday present I head to the Saturday seasonal art and crafts market on spacious Kongens Nytorv square, where a small collection of trestle tables are laden with silverware, canvases, memorabilia and vintage Royal Copenhagen porcelain. Many of the plates and mugs are emblazoned with dates, and you can have fun finding a piece with your, or your loved one's birth year on it. As well as the signature pattern – white with cobalt-blue geometric plant motifs – you might find striking multi-coloured pieces with bold designs, rather than the more traditional rustic or family scenes.

Come mid-November, the square transforms into a thoroughly hygge daily Christmas market, where you can wander the sparkly stalls and sip mulled wine with cardamom and almonds (gløgg) and, if you're so inclined, eat traditional festive flaeskesteg (roast pork).

Veras Market

Catch Danish sartorial style at this chic street market.

Under Bispeengbuen Bridge, connecting Frederiksberg and Nørrebro

Fuglebakken / Nørrebro

Sun 11am–4pm (Apr–Oct)

verascopenhagen.dk

Strolling around the city streets you might begin to feel just a bit envious of the effortless boho chic of the bike-riding locals. You can find Danish style at budget prices by heading to hip hangout Veras Market which, like all the flea markets in this chilly city, only opens in the warmer months and only on Sundays, so head here if you're in the city on a weekend.

This is where local fashionistas ditch their (still gorgeous) garments as styles change, and you can pick up some amazing bargains from more than eighty outdoor stalls. Styles tend to the colourful and flamboyant, rather than toned-down Scandi cool. You can also clothes-swap here. Musicians from the Sound of Copenhagen label perform in the lounge area, and food trucks dish out coffee and snacks. The market switches to an indoor location in winter – see the website for details.

Must-buys + markets

Jægersborggade

*The best shopping street in the city, from crafts and
eco-wares to vintage fashion and vinyl.*

It's a big challenge to walk down Jægersborggade and not buy anything;
the tall pastel-hued buildings house the most interesting stores in town.

I like to food shop at LØS Market (no.20), a refill store selling organic
grains, nuts and vegetables. My Favourite Things (no.44) also flies the eco-
flag, with organic and green-friendly beauty products and accessories.

At Palermo Hollywood (no.31) you'll find beautiful upcycled garments;
there's a stylish and personal collection of handmade and Fairtrade jewellery,
ceramics, art and clothing at Vanishing Point (no.45); while the jewellery at
collective Ladyfingers (no.4) is a good choice for a chic gift. Crate Beer and
Vinyl (no.50) sells, you guessed it, beer and second-hand records (including
some underground Danish hip hop); Wilgart (no.10) features handmade caps;
while weirdly appealing Beyond Coffee (no.35) specialises in grow-your-own
mushroom kits, fuelled by discarded coffee grounds.

The street is also dotted with great places to eat: try the pastry
confections at Meyers Bageri (no.9), sugar-free vegan-but-creamy banana
ice-cream at Banana (no.27), sensational seasonal food at Manfreds (no.40;
see p.57) or have a barista-style brew at the Coffee Collective (no.57). If
you're in town at the beginning of December, look out for Jægersborggade's
Christmas event, where stores sell festive gifts and dish up pretzels and
glasses of port to shoppers.

Jægersborggade   Hours vary

Nørrebros Runddel

Must-buys + markets

Muttilove

Ultra-feminine and funky upcycled clothes for women.

Birkegade 9
26 18 15 97

5C

Mon 12pm–6pm
Tues–Fri 11am–6pm
Sat 11am–4pm

W
muttilove.dk

Cute, quirky and loveable, Muttilove is a passion project that brands itself as 'feminine slow fashion'. Owner Karen takes off-cuts and discarded materials and personally crafts them into distinctive garments which, with their padded shoulders and nipped-in waists, emphasise womanly curves. Muttilove steers clear of being too girly though, with the use of zips and sharp tailoring, which give the clothes a slightly formidable edge.

Karen will demonstrate how to layer her bright creations: bolero jackets, swirling full skirts and warming sleeveless jackets. Although the shapes are standardised, the fabric is not, so if you buy something here it really will be one of a kind.

Nip next door to BauBau (see p.175) for men's clothing.

BauBau

Designer clothes for men at bargain prices.

Birkegade 3

40 86 29 37

5C

Mon–Fri 11am–6pm

Sat 11am–4pm

W

baubaushop.com

BauBau is a gem, a second-hand clothes store that specialises in designer garb and, as owner Casper puts it, 'the random brandless, vintage oddities that tell a story and embody something I believe to be cool and/or beautiful.' The word curated is overused, but this really is a beautifully curated and very personal store.

As far as labels go, have a rummage and you're likely to turn up pieces by Jil Sander, Alexander McQueen, Comme des Garçons, Prada, Dries van Noten, Yohji Yamamoto and many more star names. You might also find Scandi brands such as Jean//phillip, Acne and Soulland. BauBau's ultra-cool but friendly shop assistants are great at fashion suggestions and sizing advice. For women, Muttilove (see p.174) is right next door.

Must-buys + markets

Less a Fair

A one-stop shop for beautiful, sustainable goods.

After a brunch at Souls (see p.59), head into the bright and welcoming Less a Fair eco-shop, whose mantra is 'less waste, more love'. Around a third of the shop is devoted to a second-hand clothing section, which fits neatly with the sustainable ethos. The rest of the store features artisanal products, from jute slip-on shoes to beautiful kimonos by Habiba Salon, inspired by artists and stars such as Yoko Ono and Milla Jovovich.

You'll find pretty much everything you need for green living here: face and body products, kitchen and bathroom items, throw rugs, candles and furniture, plus underwear, woollen items, bags, purses and jewellery.

My personal favourite is the Relove and Roses brand: vintage fabrics and Indian saris transformed into beautiful clothing and accessories. And the poppy red, pomegranate and coral Manucurist nail varnishes – improbably made with potato, wheat, cassava, corn, bamboo and coconut oil – are deeply gorgeous.

Nordre Frihavnsgade 76

Tues–Fri 11am–5.30pm
Sat 11am–3pm

lessafair.dk

Trianglen

Must-buys + markets

Den Blå Hal

Search for Scandi homewares at this huge flea market.

This weekly flea market is located in an anonymous white warehouse building out on Amager, but is well worth the trip for those who love diving for second-hand treasures. You'll find 100 stalls, purveying everything from mid-century chairs, glass lamps and ornate clocks to Chinoiserie tea dresses to gilt-framed paintings and curios. On my last visit I spied a gorgeous egg-yolk yellow porcelain vase, a vintage silk Italian scarf, funky winged trainers, some covetable jade green pottery and an accordion!

The porcelain collections here are wonderful, making it a good spot to find bargains on Royal Copenhagen pieces (see p.163). And music lovers will enjoy exploring the eclectic vinyl on display, alongside turntables and electric guitars. If you see something you fancy but don't like the price, it's standard practice here to try a bit of bartering.

Even if you don't plan to buy, walking round the market is a fun education in the history of Danish homewares. And there's a hyggelige in-house cafe to give you a break from rummaging, serving very affordable traditional smørrebrød (open sandwiches), burgers and drinks.

Ved Amagerbanen 9	Sat–Sun 10am–4pm	**DKK** Entrance 10
Lergravsparken / Øresund		**W** denblaahal.dk

Must-buys + markets

Louisiana, on the shores of Øresund sea, makes for a really special daytrip. In summer I always go for a dip in the water, which laps at the shoreline of the gallery, and some evenings there are events and performances to keep you here until nightfall. Unmissable is an overused term, but it fits lovely Louisiana perfectly.

The original villa housing the Louisiana Museum of Modern Art has been extended, with long, low Japanese-style 1950s buildings enhancing the harmony and balance of the place. The lovely low-rise circular galleries are a hymn both to modernist architecture and – with a stunning seaside setting and large well-established trees – the great Scandinavian outdoors. The 40-minute train trip north from the city centre to the low-key town of Humlebæk is part of the pleasure, as is wandering the grassed surroundings dotted with reclining figures by Henry Moore and playful outdoor murals by Alexander Calder.

Inside are works by an array of art superstars – Picasso, Andy Warhol, Rothko and more – while temporary shows take you to the cutting-edge of video and installation art: these exhibitions are often politically charged and powerful. The natural surroundings are woven into the experience throughout, with Giacometti sculptures and Francis Bacon paintings set against plunging picture windows framing tall pine trees and impossibly green lawns.

Louisiana's cafe does brisk business selling hearty filled rolls and pastries, and there's a next-level gallery store with a chic clothing selection for men and women, plus art books, ceramics and jewellery.

GETTING THERE

Approximate time and distance from Copenhagen: one hour (35 km/21 miles).

By train: From København H (Central) station, trains run north along the coast and take about 35 minutes. Once at Humlebæk station, follow the signs for the tranquil 10-minute walk to the museum.

By bus: Bus 388 runs from Copenhagen to Humlebæk but the train is quicker and easier.

Cycling: The coastal road (152) will get you from Copenhagen to Louisiana in around two hours.

Driving: Take the E47/E55 roads, which run north along the sound for an easy 30-minute drive to the museum. There's free parking onsite.

Sitting on the shore in the town of Roskilde, the Viking Ship Museum tells a wonderfully dramatic Danish tale. At the heart of the experience are five reconstructed Viking ships. You can become a Viking for a day too, sailing on the harbour in a longboat.

The sight of the five ancient ships here is unforgettable. The ships were deliberately scuppered way back in 1070, to serve as hidden sea defences against enemy attack and part of the drama of this museum is the story of their discovery in 1962. The surrounding galleries are full of colour and detail about the process of restoration and Viking life, some of it bloodcurdlingly violent. And you can step onboard a model of a longboat, which gives you a strong sense of life on the ocean.

The neighbouring boatyard is part of the museum: here, skilled builders created facsimiles of the ships around 15 years ago and tested their seaworthiness. The yard has lots of activities for adults and children, such as rope-making and Norse dress-ups. And there's also a terrific cafe serving (vaguely) Viking fare: they avoid potatoes, tomatoes and cucumbers, which the infamous marauders had no access to, and instead serve flatbread and cook with pearl barley, sea buckthorn and angelica.

The key experience here is to set sail on the harbour, either in a reconstructed longboat or a Danish fishing boat, the design of which has changed little in 800 years. You'll be expected to play your part as a sailor, helping to row the boat into the bay and hauling ropes to hoist the sail. It's a thrilling and very physical experience. Tickets are sold for the daily one-hour trips (May–Sept) on a first-come, first-served basis from 10am; sailings run into the early afternoon. They're suitable for children over age four; there is no disabled access.

The maritime setting of the museum is very evocative, but sadly the sea has become too close for comfort, and recently the Viking ships found themselves lapped with water once more during severe flooding. There are plans to rebuild the museum in a safer spot, so check in advance before you visit, see: vikingeskibsmuseet.dk/en.

GETTING THERE

By train: It's a 30-minute train trip from København H (Central) station to Roskilde and the museum is a 20-minute walk from the station. If you don't want to walk, take bus 203 or a taxi – there are usually several at the station.
Cycling: The minor 156 road provides cyclists with a straightforward route; the ride will take just under two hours from Copenhagen (30 km/18 miles).
Driving: Follow route 21, which runs west from Copenhagen to Roskilde: it'll take around 30 minutes to reach the museum. There's free parking onsite.

Daytrip

The ARKEN Museum for Moderne Kunst (Museum of Modern Art) is a thoroughly unexpected attraction: a cathedral to modern art in a remote location by grass-edged dunes. For anyone interested in the bleeding edge of modern Danish and international art, including video art and installations, the daytrip to this museum on tranquil Køge Bay is well worth making.

In its permanent collection, ARKEN displays works that were mostly created from the 1990s onwards. Artists featured include Damien Hirst, Olafur Eliasson, Wolfgang Tillmans, Ai Weiwei and Anselm Reyle. Temporary exhibits might comprise ambitious video work and elaborate large-scale installations, as well as homages to major artists like Picasso.

The building itself, constructed in 1996, is part of the adventure – it's a high white triangular structure that references the hull of a ship. And the contents merit at least half a day of your time.

Take a break at ARKEN's cafe, which hangs like a lifeboat from the bay side of the building and serves fish, vegetable and meat platters, plus brunch, sandwiches and cakes. The museum shop displays exclusive lithographs and Nordic design pieces, alongside quirky gifts, art books and magazines.

After your gallery visit, there are walks on lovely Ishøj beach, which stretches for seven sandy kilometres; there's a wooden pier to jump into the sea from and a lifeguard here in summer.

GETTING THERE

By train: Take the train from København H (Central) station to Ishøj station (22 minutes) and then hop onto the 128 bus to Køge Bay (7 minutes). You can also walk on paths from the station to the gallery – that will take around 20 minutes.

Cycling: A cross-country ride west on the 151 road will get cyclists from Copenhagen to Arken in around an hour (16 km/30 miles).

Driving: The E20 from Copenhagen takes drivers across to Amager and then down the coast to Arken. Driving takes about 25 minutes. There's free parking at the museum.

Daytrip

THE ESSENTIALS

Copenhagen is a well-organised city and one that is easy to navigate. Danes generally speak wonderful English, so it's very easy to quickly feel at home. These tips will help you travel like a local.

GETTING TO COPENHAGEN

Plane

Copenhagen's airport, Kastrup, is located just south of the city on Amager island. It's a very quick journey from the airport to the centre: around 15 minutes. If you're going to København H (Central) station then the train is the best option transport-wise, while for districts such as Christianshavn, Østerbro, Nørrebro and Vesterbro, it's best to hop on the metro.

Train

It's surprisingly easy and pleasurable, as well as much more environmentally friendly, to travel to Copenhagen by train from major European cities. With an early start, it's possible to do the trip even from London in a (long) day. Alternatively, travel from London to Brussels or Hamburg and stay overnight, and then take an onward service to Copenhagen the next day; from Brussels the journey takes twelve hours and from Hamburg five hours.

GETTING AROUND COPENHAGEN

Walking

Copenhagen is a compact city and, thanks to the number of bikes, not a car-dominated one. Walking the cobbled lanes, canals and harbour walkways is a delight.

Bike

This is the city of the bike. Copenhagen has it all figured out: bike traffic lights, separate lanes, bike bridges (see p.153) and several cycle-only routes. You can bring your bike on the train and metro (except for during rush hour). There are special carriages for them on trains (look on the ground by the platform to see if there's a bike symbol). You need to buy a ticket to bring a bike (and scooters if they are not folded) – you can add a bike (and extra people) when checking in with your Rejsekort (see p.188) ticket. The only problem you're likely to encounter is the locals' annoyance with tourists cycling slowly: the Copenhagen version of road rage. There are plenty of

The Essentials

options for flexible and affordable bike rental (see p.123).

PUBLIC TRANSPORT

Denmark uses a travel card, Rejsekort (www.rejsekort.dk) on all public transport (train, metro and bus). You can also buy tickets on your phone. I recommend downloading the app (www.rejseplanen.dk), which has a journey planner, too. Many public transport vehicles have GPS trackers, so the information is current. The Rejsekort card costs DKK 80 and can be purchased at the airport and at major train stations (such as Nørreport and København H). The card can be used throughout the whole country. There needs to be DKK 50 on it at all times (to cover the fine if you forget to check-out at the end of the journey) but you can't get any money back, so don't add too much. You can top-up on machines at most stations. Check-in (by touching on) when getting on public transport; you do this every time you change vehicles and check-out (touch off) when exiting the last vehicle/station. Most train, metro and bus stops will have a digital display that shows how long until the next transport arrives (there will be a list with the stops), and many vehicles (including most buses) have displays inside that show you the next stop – making it easy to know when to get off. If you're only in Copenhagen for a couple of days the Copenhagen Card (see p.189) gives access to public transport, so this could be a better option.

Boat

Yellow harbour bus boats (see p.91) run up and down the main waterway from north to south, with plenty of stopping-off points along the way. They are rapid and cheap, costing the same as a bus, and you can wheel your bike onboard.

LIVE LIKE A LOCAL

Hygge life

Throughout this guide I've recommended experiences, restaurants, bars and shops that embody the Danish quality of hygge. The word's most literal translation is 'cosy', but it implies much more: warmth, friendship, communality and relaxed comfort.

Danish language

Listening to the Danish language and seeing it written down, you'll be heartily relieved that the locals speak English to an excellent standard. The language has three additional letters: Æ (a sliding combination of 'a' and 'e', like the 'e' in 'enter'), Ø (pronounced like the 'ir' in 'weird'), and Å (like the 'o' in 'oh'). One word that you might like to wrap your mouth around, as you're likely to order it a fair bit, is smørrebrød: pronounced something like smuhr-bruth and meaning a traditional open sandwich.

Useful phrases

Hello – Hej
Good morning – God morgen
Good day – God dag
Good night – Godnat
Goodbye – Hej hej/Farvel
How are you? – Hvordan går det?
I'm well, and you? – Godt, hvad med dig?
Good, thanks – Godt, tak!
My name is ... – Jeg hedder ... or – mit navn er ...
Yes – Ja
No – Nej
How do you say ... in Danish? – Hvordan siger du ... på dansk?
Thank you – Tak
You're welcome – Selv tak or det var sa lidt
How much is it? – Hvor meget koster det?
Where is ... – Hvor er...
What's your name? – Hvad hedder du?
Where are you from? – Hvor kommer du fra?
I'm from ... – Jeg er fra ...
What time is it? – Hvad er klokken?
I'm looking for ... – Jeg leder efter ...

MUSEUMS AND SIGHTS

Nearly all the major sights close on Mondays, so make plans for outdoor activities on that day.

Copenhagen Card

If you're doing lots of sightseeing it's well worth buying a Copenhagen Card, which includes free entry to 87 museums and free transport in the wider Copenhagen region. You can buy 24-, 48-, 72- or 120-hour cards. Purchase the cards online (copenhagencard.com) or at tourist board offices. The main office, which has a wealth of maps and information, is at Vesterbrogade 4.

Discount tickets

Entry to museums is not cheap in Copenhagen, and there are usually no reductions for senior citizens, although students will get discounts of around 25 per cent, and those under 18 years old get reductions or free entry.

DINING IN COPENHAGEN

Smørrebrød and snaps

Danes really love smørrebrød: open sandwiches where the freshest of fish, herbs and leaves sit prettily on rye bread. There are also meat and vegetarian alternatives: in fact, pretty much any combination you can think of will be dished up, and smørrebrød is eaten for lunch and dinner. The tradition is to serve smørrebrød with a dainty triangular glass of snaps spirit, often aquavit, which is distilled from grain and potatoes, and flavoured with herbs and spices.

THE ESSENTIALS

There is an increasingly strong interest in super-seasonal and sustainable food, sometimes termed New Nordic cuisine, which across the board is of a very good quality.

Lunch is generally eaten around 12pm, and dinner from 6pm.

Natural wine and craft beer
The twin obsessions of the city are natural organic wine (refreshingly hangover-free) and super-local craft beer, often made using esoteric seasonal ingredients. Skål! (Cheers!)

Tipping
It's not really expected or the custom to tip, as Danish companies pay a good living wage. Fine-dining restaurants are the exceptions, where, paradoxically, wages tend to be lower, and it's good practise to tip 10–15 per cent if you were satisfied with the meal and service.

SEASONS AND DATES
The climate is not the reason you come to Denmark. The hottest month is July, with average highs of 17°C (63°F). July and August can be wonderful, with warm temperatures and long bright days, when the sun dips down after 11pm. Chilly January has average highs of 0°C (32°F), and throughout winter the days are short, dark, damp and sometimes it snows; the sun sets just after 3.30pm.

This is just a taster of some of the celebrations and events to be enjoyed throughout the year in Copenhagen.

Vinterjazz
For nearly the whole month of February, this jazz-loving city gets its groove on with concerts in venues large and small. There's also a ten-day jazz festival in July. See: jazz.dk

3DaysofDesign
Held in late May/early June, this design festival celebrates Danish style with exhibitions, talks and tours. See: 3daysofdesign.dk

CHP Opera Festival
This inclusive and lively event is held in July and August and brings opera to locations ranging from boats to warehouses. See: operafestival.dk

Cooking and Food Festival
There's a strong emphasis on sustainability and seasonal eating at this ten-day food festival held in August, with cooking demonstrations, tours and communal meals at long trestle tables. See: copenhagencooking.com

Christmas and New Year
Winter is a hygge time, with markets, warming gløgg (mulled wine), skating rinks and festive sparkling lights. New Year is celebrated in the City Hall Square and by the lakes with fireworks,

poppers and firecrackers, and at midnight Danes literally jump into the year, from a chair or any other raised surface.

PRACTICALITIES

Currency

The Danish currency is the krone. The coins, with wave patterns, hearts and holes punched through them, are very attractive. The currency is pegged against the euro: the DKK 100 note is equivalent to around €14. Cash machines (ATMs) are easy to find, but it's also easy just to use a debit or credit card for most transactions.

Phones and Wi-Fi

Copenhagen is a well-connected and future-facing city, so you should have no problems making calls or getting online. As with most European cities, you can purchase a local SIM card or pay for data roaming with your local service provider. Some companies give free SIM cards at the airport.